WALKS ROUND
PARIS

Titles in the Footpaths of Europe Series

Normandy and the Seine
Walking through Brittany
Walks in Provence
Coastal Walks: Normandy and Brittany
Walking the Pyrenees
Walks in the Auvergne
Walks in the Dordogne
Walks in the Loire Valley
Walking the GR5: Modane to Larche
Walking the GR5: Lake Geneva to Mont-Blanc
Paris to Boulogne
Walks in Corsica
Walking the GR5: Larche to Nice
Walking the GR5: Vosges to Jura
Walks in the Cévennes
Walks round Paris
Walking in France: The GR System

The publishers thank the following people for permission to use their
photographs in this book: J Cantaloube, Philippe Lambert.

WALKS ROUND
PARIS

Translated by Mike Parry

Robertson McCarta

The publishers thank the following people for their help with this book: Isabelle Daguin, Philippe Lambert, Serge Sineux, Jane Hawksley.

First published in 1991 by

Robertson McCarta Limited
17-18 Angel Gate
City Road
London EC1V 2PT

in association with

Fédération Française de la Randonnée Pédestre
8 Avenue Marceau
75008 Paris

© Robertson McCarta Limited
© Fédération Française de la Randonnée Pédestre
© Maps, Institut Geographique National (French Official Survey)
  and Robertson McCarta Limited.

Managing Editor Folly Marland
Series designed by Prue Bucknall
Production by Grahame Griffiths
Typeset by The Robertson Group, Llandudno
Origination by Toppan Limited
Planning Map by Rodney Paull

Printed and bound in Italy by Grafedit S.p.A. Bergamo.

British Library Cataloguing in Publication Data

Walks round Paris. – (Footpaths of Europe).
    1. France. Paris – Visitors' guides
    914.436

    ISBN 1-85365-234-2

Every care has been taken to ensure that all the information in this book is accurate. The publishers cannot accept any responsibility for any errors that may appear or their consequences.

CONTENTS

The walks and maps

Walk 1

GR1 **La Porte Maillot** ▶ Saint-Cloud ▶ Triel-sur-Seine ▶ L'Isle-Adam
▶ Meaux ▶ Melun ▶ Malesherbes ▶ Dourdan ▶ Feucherolles
▶ St Germain-en-Laye ▶ **Achères-Ville**

Walk 2

GR1A Viarmes ▶ Boran-sur-Oise ▶ **Saint-Leu-d'Esserent**

Walk 3

GR1B **Gare D'Isles-Armentières-Congis** ▶ Varreddes ▶ Cregy-les-Meaux
▶ Meaux

Walk 4

GR1C **Poigny-la-Forêt** ▶ Auffargis ▶ La Maison de Fer
▶ **Maincourt-sur-Yvette**

Walk 5

GR1C Marines ▶ Brignancourt ▶ Chars *GR1C*

Key to IGN Maps

Motorway, dual carriageway _____

Major road, four lanes or more _____

Main road, two-lane or three-lane, wide _____

Main road, two-lane, narrow _____

Narrow road, regularly surfaced _____

Other narrow road: regularly surfaced; irregularly surfaced _____

Possibly private or controlled access

Field track, forest track, felling track, footpath _____

Track of disused road. Road under construction _____

Road through embankment, cutting. Tree-lined road or track _____

Bank. Hedge, line of trees _____

Railway: double track, single track. Electrified line. Station, waiting line. Halt, stop _____

Sidings or access lines. Narrow gauge line. Rack railway _____

Electricity transmission line. Cable railway. Ski lift _____

National boundary with markers _____

Boundary and administrative centre of department, district _____ PF _____ SP

Boundary and administrative centre of canton, commune _____ CT _____ C

For shooting times, go to town hall or gendarmerie

Boundary of military camp, firing range _____

Boundary of State forest, National Park, outer zone of National Park _____

Triangulation points _____

Church, chapel, shrine. Cross, tomb, religious statue. Cemetery _____

Watch tower, fortress. Windmill, wind-pump. Chimney _____ Tr   Chem.

Storage tank: oil, gas. Blast furnace. Pylon. Quarry _____

Cave. Monument, pillar. Castle. Ruins _____ Mon.   P.V.

Megalithic monument: dolmen, menhir. Viewpoint. Campsite _____

Market-hall, shed, glasshouse. casemate _____

Access to underground workings. Refuge. Ski-jump _____ Mine   Cave

Population/thousands _____ 183,2   0,4   0,15   0,06

Bridge. Footbridge. Ford. Ferry _____

Lake, pool. Area liable to flooding. Marsh _____

Source, spring. Well, water-tank. Water-tower, reservoir _____ Ch⁻ d'Eau

Watercourse lined with trees. Waterfall. Dam. Dyke _____

Navigable canal, feeder or irrigator. Lock, machine-operated. Underground channel

Contour lines, 10 m. interval. Hollow. Small basin. Scree _____

Principal — Secondary

Woodland   Scrub   Orchard, plantation   Vines   Ricefield

All maps are IGN Orange series, 1:50 000

© I.G.N. – Paris

A note from the publisher

The books in this French Walking Guide series are produced in association and with the help of the Fédération Française de la Randonnée Pédestre (French Ramblers' Association) — generally known as the FFRP.

The FFRP is a federal organisation and is made up of regional, local and many other associations and bodies that form its constituent parts. Individual membership is through these various local organisations. The FFRP therefore acts as an umbrella organisation overseeing the waymarking of footpaths, training and the publishing of the Topoguides, detailed guides to the Grande Randonnée footpaths.

There are at present about 170 Topoguides in print, compiled and written by local members of the FFRP, who are responsible for waymarking the walks — so they are well researched and accurate.

We have translated the main itinerary descriptions, amalgamating and adapting several Topoguides to create new regional guides. We have retained the basic Topoguide structure, indicating length and times of walks, and the Institut Géographique National (French official Survey) maps overlaid with the routes.

The information contained in this guide is the latest available at the time of going to print. However, as publishers we are aware that this kind of information is continually changing and we are anxious to enhance and improve the guides as much as possible. We encourage you to send us suggestions, criticisms and those little bits of information you may wish to share with your fellow walkers. Our address is: Robertson McCarta, 17-18 Angel Gate, City Road, London EC1V 2PT.

We shall be happy to offer a free copy of any one of these books to any reader whose suggestions are subsequently incorporated into a new edition.

It is possible to create a variety of routes by referring to the walks in the contents page and to the planning map (inside the front cover). Transport is listed in the alphabetical index in the back of the book and there is an accommodation guide.

The full range of IGN (French OS) maps is available from The Map and Guide Shop, who operate a mail order service, 17-18 Angel Gate, City Road, London EC1V 2PT, Tel: 071 278 8276

KEY

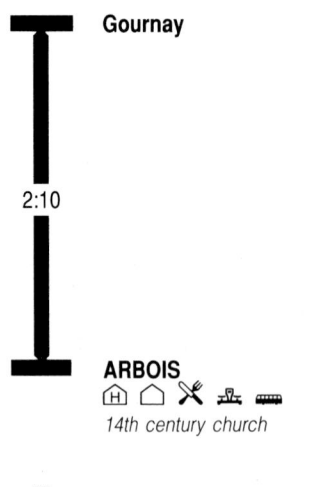

Gournay

This example shows that you can expect the walk from Gournay to Arbois to take 2 hours, 10 minutes.

2:10

ARBOIS

14th century church

Arbois has a variety of facilities, including hotels and buses. Hotel addresses and bus/train connections may be listed in the index at the back of the book.

A grey arrow indicates an alternative route that leaves and returns to the main route.

Detour

indicates a short detour off the route to a town with facilities or to an interesting sight.

Symbols:

⌂	hotel	⚒	shops
⌂	youth hostel, hut or refuge	🚂	railway station
⛺	camping	🚌	buses
✗	restaurant	⛴	ferry
☿	cafe	🄱	tourist information

THE FOOTPATHS OF FRANCE

by Robin Neillands

Why should you go walking in France? Well, walking is fun and as for France, Danton summed up the attractions of that country with one telling phrase: 'Every man has two countries,' he said, 'his own . . . and France.' That is certainly true in my case and I therefore consider it both a pleasure and an honour to write this general introduction to these footpath guides to France. A pleasure because walking in or through France is my favourite pastime, an honour because these excellent English language guides follow in the course set by those Topoguides published in French by the Fédération Française de la Randonnée Pédestre, which set a benchmark for quality that all footpath guides might follow. Besides, I believe that good things should be shared and walking in France is one of the most pleasant activities I know.

I have been walking in France for over thirty years. I began by rambling — or rather ambling — through the foothills of the Pyrenees, crossing over into Spain past the old Hospice de France, coming back over the Somport Pass in a howling blizzard, which may account for the fact that I totally missed two sets of frontier guards on both occasions. Since then I have walked in many parts of France and even from one end of it to the other, from the Channel to the Camargue, and I hope to go on walking there for many years to come.

The attractions of France are legion, but there is no finer way to see and enjoy them than on foot. France has two coasts, at least three mountain ranges — the Alps, Pyrenees and the Massif Central — an agreeable climate, a great sense of space, good food, fine wines and, believe it or not, a friendly and hospitable people. If you don't believe me, go there on foot and see for yourself. Walking in France will appeal to every kind of walker, from the day rambler to the backpacker, because above all, and in the nicest possible way, the walking in France is well organised, but those Francophiles who already know France well will find it even more pleasurable if they explore their favourite country on foot.

The GR system

The Grande Randonnée (GR) footpath network now consists of more than 40,000 kilometres (25,000 miles) of long-distance footpath, stretching into every part of France, forming a great central sweep around Paris, probing deeply into the Alps, the Pyrenees, and the volcanic cones of the Massif Central. This network, the finest system of footpaths in Europe, is the creation of that marvellously named organisation, *la Fédération Française de la Randonnée Pédestre, Comité National des Sentiers de Grande Randonnée*, which I shall abbreviate to FFRP-CNSGR. Founded in 1948, and declaring that, *'un jour de marche, huit jours de santé'*, the FFRP-CNSGR has flourished for four decades and put up the now familiar red-and-white waymarkers in every corner of the country. Some of these footpaths are classic walks, like the famous GR65, *Le Chemin de St. Jacques,* the ancient Pilgrim Road to Compostela, the TMB, the *Tour du Mont Blanc,* which circles the mountain through France, Switzerland and Italy, or the 600-mile long GR3, the *Sentier de la Loire,* which runs from the Ardèche to the Atlantic, to give three examples from the hundred or so GR trails available. In addition there is an abundance of GR du Pays or regional footpaths, like the *Sentier de la Haute Auvergne,* and the *Sentier Tour des Monts d'Aubrac.* A 'Tour' incidentally, is usually a

9

circular walk. Many of these regional or provincial GR trails are charted and waymarked in red-and-yellow by local outdoor organisations such as ABRI (Association Bretonne des Relais et Itineraires) for Brittany, or CHAMINA for the Massif Central. The walker in France will soon become familiar with all these footpath networks, national, regional or local, and find them the perfect way into the heart and heartland of France. As a little bonus, the GR networks are expanding all the time, with the detours — or *varientes* — off the main route eventually linking with other GR paths or *varientes* and becoming GR trails in their own right.

Walkers will find the GR trails generally well marked and easy to follow, and they have two advantages over the footpaths commonly encountered in the UK. First, since they are laid out by local people, they are based on intricate local knowledge of the local sights. If there is a fine view, a mighty castle or a pretty village on your footpath route, your footpath through France will surely lead you to it. Secondly, all French footpaths are usually well provided with a wide range of comfortable country accommodation, and you will discover that the local people, even the farmers, are well used to walkers and greet them with a smile, a *'Bonjour'* and a *'bonne route'*.

Terrain and Climate
As a glance at these guides or any Topoguide will indicate, France has a great variety of terrain. France is twice the size of the UK and many natural features are also on a larger scale. There are three main ranges of mountains, the Alps contain the highest mountain in Europe, the Pyrenees go up to 10,000 ft, the Massif Central peaks to over 6000 ft, and there are many similar ranges with hills which overtop our highest British peak, Ben Nevis. On the other hand, the Auvergne and the Jura have marvellous open ridge walking, the Cévennes are steep and rugged, the Ardèche and parts of Provence are hot and wild, the Île-de-France, Normandy, Brittany and much of western France is green and pleasant, not given to extremes. There is walking in France for every kind of walker, but given such a choice the wise walker will consider the complications of terrain and weather before setting out, and go suitably equipped.

France enjoys three types of climate: continental, oceanic, and Mediterranean. South of the Loire it will certainly be hot to very hot from mid-April to late September. Snow can fall on the mountains above 4000 ft from mid-October and last until May, or even lie year-round on the tops and in couloirs; in the high hills an ice-axe is never a frill. I have used one by the Brèche de Roland in the Pyrenees in mid-June.

Wise walkers should study weather maps and forecasts carefully in the week before they leave for France, but can generally expect good weather from May to October, and a wide variety of weather — the severity depending on the terrain — from mid-October to late Spring.

Accommodation
The walker in France can choose from a wide variety of accommodation with the assurance that the walker will always be welcome. This can range from country hotels to wild mountain pitches, but to stay in comfort, many walkers will travel light and overnight in the comfortable hotels of the *Logis de France* network.

Logis de France: The *Logis de France* is a nationwide network of small, family-run country hotels, offering comfortable accommodation and excellent food. *Logis* hotels are graded and can vary from a simple, one-star establishment, with showers and linoleum, to a four- or five-star *logis* with gastronomic menus and deep pile carpets. All offer excellent value for money, and since there are over 5,000 scattered across the French countryside, they provide a good focus for a walking day. An annual guide to the *Logis* is available from the French Government Tourist Office, 178 Piccadilly, London W1V 0AL, Tel (071) 491 7622.

Gîtes d'étape: A *gîte d'étape* is best imagined as an unmanned youth hostel for outdoor folk of all ages. They lie along the footpath networks and are usually signposted or listed in the guides. They can be very comfortable, with bunk beds, showers, a well equipped kitchen, and in some cases they have a warden, a *guardien,* who may offer meals. *Gîtes d'étape* are designed exclusively for walkers, climbers, cyclists, cross-country skiers or horse-riders. A typical price (1990) would be Fr.25 for one night. *Gîtes d'étape* should not be confused with a *Gîte de France.* A *gîte* — usually signposted as *'Gîte de France'* — is a country cottage available for a holiday let, though here too, the owner may be more than willing to rent it out as overnight accommodation.

Youth hostels: Curiously enough, there are very few youth hostels in France outside the main towns. A full list of the 200 or so available can be obtained from the Youth Hostel Association (YHA), Trevelyan House, St. Albans, Herts AL1 2DY.

Pensions or cafes: In the absence of an hotel, a *gîte d'étape* or a youth hostel, all is not lost. France has plenty of accommodation and an enquiry at the village cafe or bar will usually produce a room. The cafe/hotel may have rooms or suggest a nearby pension or a *chambre d'hôte.* Prices start at around Fr.50 for a room, rising to say, Fr.120 (1990 estimate).

Chambres d'hôte: A *chambre d'hôte* is a guest room, or, in English terms, a bed-and-breakfast, usually in a private house. Prices range from about Fr.90 a night. *Chambres d'hôte* signs are now proliferating in the small villages of France and especially if you can speak a little French are an excellent way to meet the local people. Prices (1990) are from, say, Fr.70 for a room, not per person.

Abris: Abris, shelters or mountain huts can be found in the mountain regions, where they are often run by the Club Alpin Français, an association for climbers. They range from the comfortable to the primitive, are often crowded and are sometimes reserved for members. Details from the Club Alpin Français, 7 Rue la Boétie, Paris 75008, France.

Camping: French camp sites are graded from one to five star, but are generally very good at every level, although the facilities naturally vary from one cold tap to shops, bars and heated pools. Walkers should not be deterred by the *'Complet'* (Full) sign on the gate or office window: a walker's small tent will usually fit in somewhere. *Camping à la ferme,* or farm camping, is increasingly popular, more primitive — or less regimented — than the official sites, but widely available and perfectly adequate. Wild camping is officially not permitted in National Parks, but unofficially if you are over 1,500m away from a road, one hour's walk from a *gîte* or camp site, and where possible ask permission, you should have no trouble. French country people will always assist the walker to find a pitch.

The law for walkers
The country people of France seem a good deal less concerned about their 'rights' than the average English farmer or landowner. I have never been ordered off land in France or greeted with anything other than friendliness . . . maybe I've been lucky. As

a rule, walkers in France are free to roam over all open paths and tracks. No decent walker will leave gates open, trample crops or break down walls, and taking fruit from gardens or orchards is simply stealing. In some parts of France there are local laws about taking chestnuts, mushrooms (and snails), because these are cash crops. Signs like *Réserve de Chasse,* or *Chasse Privé* indicate that the shooting is reserved for the landowner. As a general rule, behave sensibly and you will be tolerated everywhere, even on private land.

The country code
Walkers in France should obey the Code du Randonneur.

- Love and respect nature.
- Avoid unnecessary noise.
- Destroy nothing.
- Do not leave litter.
- Do not pick flowers or plants.
- Do not disturb wildlife.
- Re-close all gates.
- Protect and preserve the habitat.
- No smoking or fires in the forests. (This rule is essential and is actively enforced by foresters and police.)
- Respect and understand the country way of life and the country people.
- Think of others as you think of yourself.

Transport
Transportation to and within France is generally excellent. There are no less than nine Channel ports: Dunkirk, Calais, Boulogne, Dieppe, Le Havre, Caen/Ouistreham, Cherbourg, Saint-Malo and Roscoff, and a surprising number of airports served by direct flights from the UK. Although some of the services are seasonal, it is often possible to fly direct to Toulouse, Poitiers, Nantes, Perpignan, Montpellier, indeed to many provincial cities, as well as Paris and such obvious destinations as Lyon and Nice. Within France the national railway, the SNCF, still retains a nationwide network. Information, tickets and a map can be obtained from the SNCF. France also has a good country bus service and the *gare routière* is often placed just beside the railway station. Be aware though, that many French bus services only operate within the *département,* and they do not generally operate from one provincial city to the next. I cannot encourage people to hitch-hike, which is both illegal and risky, but walkers might consider a taxi for their luggage. Almost every French village has a taxi driver who will happily transport your rucksacks to the next night-stop, fifteen to twenty miles away, for Fr.50 a head or even less.

Money
Walking in France is cheap, but banks are not common in the smaller villages, so carry a certain amount of French money and the rest in traveller's cheques or Eurocheques, which are accepted everywhere.

Clothing and equipment
The amount of clothing and equipment you will need depends on the terrain, the length of the walk, the time of your visit, the accommodation used. Outside the mountain areas it is not necessary to take the full range of camping or backpacking gear. I once

walked across France from the Channel to the Camargue along the Grande Randonneé footpaths in March, April and early May and never needed to use any of the camping gear I carried in my rucksack because I found hotels everywhere, even in quite small villages.

Essential items are:
In summer: light boots, a hat, shorts, suncream, lip salve, mosquito repellent, sunglasses, a sweater, a windproof cagoule, a small first-aid kit, a walking stick.
In winter: a change of clothing, stormproof outer garments, gaiters, hat, lip salve, a companion.
In the mountains at any time: large-scale maps (1:25,000), a compass, an ice-axe. In winter, add a companion and ten-point crampons.
At any time: a phrase book, suitable maps, a dictionary, a sense of humour.

The best guide to what to take lies in the likely weather and the terrain. France tends to be informal, so there is no need to carry a jacket or something smart for the evenings. I swear by Rohan clothing, which is light, smart and functional. The three things I would never go without are light, well-broken-in boots and several pairs of loop-stitched socks, and my walking stick.

Health hazards:
Health hazards are few. France can be hot in summer, so take a full water-bottle and refill at every opportunity. A small first-aid kit is sensible, with plasters and 'mole-skin' for blisters, but since prevention is better than the cure, loop-stitched socks and flexible boots are better. Any French chemist — a pharmacie — is obliged to render first-aid treatment for a small fee. These pharmacies can be found in most villages and large towns and are marked by a green cross.
Dogs are both a nuisance and a hazard. All walkers in France should carry a walking stick to fend off aggressive curs. Rabies — la rage — is endemic and anyone bitten must seek immediate medical advice. France also possesses two types of viper, which are common in the hill areas of the south. In fairness, although I found my walking stick indispensable, I must add that in thirty years I have never even seen a snake or a rabid dog. In case of real difficulty, dial 17 for the police and the ambulance.

Food and wine
One of the great advantages with walking in France is that you can end the day with a good meal and not gain an ounce. French country cooking is generally excellent and good value for money, with the price of a four-course menu starting at about Fr.45. The ingredients for the midday picnic can be purchased from the village shops and these also sell wine. Camping-Gaz cylinders and cartridges are widely available, as is 2-star petrol for stoves. Avoid naked fires.

Preparation
The secret of a good walk lies in making adequate preparations before you set out. It pays to be fit enough to do the daily distance at the start. Much of the necessary information is contained in this guide, but if you need more, look in guidebooks or outdoor magazines, or ask friends.

The French
I cannot close this introduction without saying a few words about the French, not least

because the walker in France is going to meet rather more French people than, say, a motorist will, and may even meet French people who have never met a foreigner before. It does help if the visitor speaks a little French, even if only to say *'bonjour'* and *'Merci'* and *'S'il vous plait'*. The French tend to be formal so it pays to be polite, to say 'hello', to shake hands. I am well aware that relations between France and England have not always been cordial over the last six hundred years or so, but I have never met with hostility of any kind in thirty years of walking through France. Indeed, I have always found that if the visitor is prepared to meet the French halfway, they will come more than halfway to greet him or her in return, and are both friendly and hospitable to the passing stranger.

As a final tip, try smiling. Even in France, or especially in France, a smile and a *'pouvez vous m'aider?'* (can you help me?) will work wonders. That's my last bit of advice, and all I need do now is wish you *'Bonne Route'* and good walking in France.

WALKS ROUND PARIS

André de Gouvenain

I f anyone were to ask me the best way of getting to know the history, geography and economic life of the Île-de-France, I would simply tell them to walk the GR1.

The 600 kilometre path winds its way around the capital through regions which vary greatly, physical geography and soil determining in each particular case the nature of local agriculture and habitat.

To understand the development of each region, however, it is necessary to take account of its history and to savour the beauty of its monuments and the charm of its country houses.

A large part of the GR1 passes through green belt country, the last remains of forests which once covered the whole of the Île-de-France. The fact that any forest remains at all is due to the kings of France, who preserved them as royal hunting grounds, and to a poor soil with excessive sand or lime, which saved them from the plough.

The GR1 sets out from Paris at the Porte Maillot, a name once spelled Mahiaulx or Mahiau, which derives from the ancient game of *mail*, a precursor of golf. Here, the path traverses woods which, in the time of the Gauls, would have been a hunting ground for bear and wolf, wild boar and deer. During the Middle Ages, the woods remained a refuge for brigands until Henri II flushed them out and enclosed the grounds with a wall to create a royal hunting park. The estate was opened to the public by Louis XVI and the grounds owe their present form to Napoleon III, who tried to create a park which would rival its models across the Channel.

Where it leaves the woods, the path crosses the Seine by a footbridge over the Avre, a river of Normandy which supplies water to the city of Paris from the reservoir of Saint-Cloud.

The route now passes close to the Pont de Saint-Cloud where, according to local legend, owners of land on the river banks used to put out nets to catch anything which the Seine might have acquired on its way downstream. The bag, apparently, would include 'ten to twelve corpses a day'.

In the Parc de Saint-Cloud, the old château was the scene of many significant events: Napoleon's coup d'état of 19 Brumaire (10 November 1799) which took place in the Orangerie; the marriage of Napoleon I and Marie-Louise in 1810; the issue of the Ordonnances of Charles X, a prelude to the revolution of 1830. The building was burned down in 1870 and demolished in 1891. The only signs of its location now are the lines of yews.

The GR1 meanders between properties until it comes to the Pavillon du Butard, Louis XV's hunting lodge, famed for receptions, organised by Paul Boivet, at which guests would be received by *nymphs* costumed in veils of white.

The route leads next to the Parc de Marly and the Tapis Vert, overlooking the site of the old Château de Marly. Seeking a quiet spot far from the bustle of Versailles, Louis XIV had a 'hermitage' built here in the ancient Forêt de Cruye, a part of the immense Forté des Yvelines which once covered the whole western side of the Île-de-France. A central pavilion reserved for the king was surrounded by 12 smaller pavilions, representing the signs of the Zodiac.

During the king's stays here - referred to as 'Marlys' - only a few courtesans were admitted, with the result, of course, that there was an abundance of intrigue. The original idea had been to recreate rustic simplicity but luxury gradually crept back.

Louis XVI was also a visitor to Marly and was there at the beginning of the French Revolution on 14 July 1789. The château, which had fallen into disrepair, was sold to the revolutionary government, which auctioned off the furniture and even the masonry.

The forest of Marly is very sandy and parts are covered with millstone grit. The terrain is rugged and there are viewpoints over the surrounding countryside. At the Étoile des Chasseurs, one branch of the GR forks off towards the forest of Saint-Germain-en-Laye. At the entry to Feucherolles, there is a junction with the GR1 coming from Rambouillet.

At Feucherolles, the path turns north and crosses the eastern part of the Mantois as far as Triel. This is a region of large-scale farming on the plateaux, orchards and copses on the slopes and market gardens in the valleys.

Near the Moulin d'Orgeval are the ruins of the old Abbaye d'Abbécourt. Between 1727 and 1732, the château at Vernouillet was the home of the Jansenist sect of 'Convulsionnaires', renowned for their performances at the cemetery of Saint-Médard in Paris.

The GR1 now continues along the right bank of the Seine, a route which it shares for a while with the GR2. A sight worth seeing at Triel is the church, which is built over the road and exhibits a number of different architectural styles. The path clings to the slope of the Bois de l'Hautil until it comes to the limestone plateau of the Vexin Français. The alluvial soil of this area is good for wheat while the valleys are more suited to animal husbandry.

Going up the valley of the Aubette through the Bois des Roches, 1.5 kilometres south of Vigny, you come to a huge quarry of oölitic limestone, a very hard rock with coral-like tubular structures.

The Château de Vigny, built in imitation of the châteaux of the Loire, has a park which is open to the public. The path leads to Us (formerly spelled Ws) and then follows the valley of the Viosne. Near to Santeuil, there is a spring of lithia water. At Marines, the 16th-century church has one of the oldest bells in France. The route now turns south east and reaches the River Oise near Pontoise.

The valley of the Oise from Pontoise to Auvers and Valmondois was much frequented by painters such as Daubigny, Cézanne, Corot and Van Gogh. The GR1 now passes by Nesles-la-Vallée, the place where the balloonists Charles and Robert landed on 1 December 1783 in their 'aérostat à gaz' after a flight of some 30 kilometres from the Tuileries.

Crossing plateaux and wooded slopes, the GR next reaches Parmain. On the other bank of the Oise lies L'Isle-Adam. The church, dating from the end of the Gothic period and the beginning of the Renaissance, is remarkable for its *voussoirs,* depicting the virtues and vices. To the north of the town, in the old Parc de Cassan, you can visit the Chinese pavilion, a *fabrique* built in 1778 after the garden fashion of that period.

The region between the Oise and the Ourcq is an agricultural area known as Parisis. Those parts where sand or grit predominates have been planted with forest, as for example at L'Isle-Adam and Carnelle. To the south of L'Isle-Adam, the GR1 crosses above the old stone quarries which now serve as mushroom farms. The path next reaches Presles, a village which, in prehistoric times, must have been an important site to judge from the scale of the 'covered avenues' nearby: La Pierre Plate (1,500 metres to the west); Blanc Val (500 metres to the south, 100 metres from the GR1); and finally the largest, La Pierre Turquaise, which is 11 kilometres long.

In the Forét de Carnelle, the path runs between the Lac Bleu and the Petit Etang, both formerly exploited as a source of fuller's earth.

From Luzarches (ancient town with keep, tower, marketplace and magnificent church with Renaissance doorway) to Dammartin-en-Goële, we are in the former 'Pays de France', an area of large-scale farming. The GR1, however, remains in the forests of Chantilly and Ermenonville, an area of the Valois described in the writings of Gérard de Nerval. It was in the Parc d'Ermenonville that the Marquis de Girardin had his various *fabriques* set up: the Dolmen, the Old Mens' Bench, the Altar of Dreams, the Temple of Philosophy, the Mothers' Table, the Queens' Bench and, on the Île des Peupliers, the tomb of the philosopher, Jean-Jacques Rousseau, who stayed as the guest of the Marquis shortly before his death.

In Merovingian times, La Goële constituted a small region of the Île-de-France, extending from Dammartin to Montgé. Beyond the village, we come to the beginning of the Multien region - through which the GR1 passes, crossing over the Buttes de Monthyon and the Buttes de Montassis before coming to Meaux. The bishops of this town, particularly Bossuet, have a notable place in French literature. In 1358, Meaux also saw the massacre of 9000 peasants during the Jacquerie.

The GR1 now passes through La Brie, another area of large-scale farming, avoiding the plateaux before coming to Crécy-la-Chapelle. Several arms of the River Grand-Morin run through the town, which is often called the 'Venice' of La Brie. Of the 99 towers which once surrounded the town, a few remain, including one where Corot lived.

The next sight is the ruined Château du Vivier, where Charles VI was kept during his fits of madness. Further on, we come to the collegiate church of Champeaux, the ruins of the castle of Blandy-les-Tours and then the Château de Vaux-le-Vicomte, built by Fouquet, Louis XIV's superintendent of finances. The path now runs through Melun, a town which, like Paris, has grown up around a fortified island. It was here that the 22 year-old Abelard set up his school of philosophy in 1101.

The forest of Fontainebleau offers some fine walks: Apremont, Franchard, Le Bois-Rond and Les Trois Pignons are all favourites of the rock-climbing fraternity.

The GR leaves the forest at Le Vaudoué, skirting woods and plateaux and occasionally passing through the small dry valleys which are typical of this part of the Gâtinais region. There are more rock faces to be seen at Auxy before the path brings you to Malesherbes. It was in the château here that Henriette, the daughter of François d'Entraigues, heeded paternal advice and 'sold her virtue' to the visiting Henri IV, receiving the handsome price of 100,000 écus and the title of Duchesse de Verneuil.

The path turns north, following the valley of the Essonne through orchards, market gardens, beds of water-cress and plantations of poplar and willow. At Boutigny, the GR leaves the Essonne and joins the valley of the Juine.

Before long, the magnificent church of Saint-Sulpice-de-Favières comes into view, dwarfing the surrounding village. For many years, the church was a place of pilgrimage in honour of Saint Sulpice. After a steep climb to the top of the Colline de Saint-Yon, there are panoramic views over the countryside. Near Saint-Chéron, the route brings you to the valley of the Orge, crossing the river at Dourdan where the castle is not to be missed.

Dourdan is the chief town of the Hurepoix, a region of plateaux and low wooded hills, lying between the forests of Fontainebleu and Rambouillet, its rivers - the Essonne, Juine, Orge and Yvette - flowing into the left bank of the Seine.

Cereals and beet are grown on the plateaux but the valleys are heavily built-up and become more so the closer they get to Paris.

The forest of Rambouillet, sandy in some parts and marshy in others, is all that remains of the vast Forêt des Yvelines which once stretched from Chevreuse to Marly.

The GR1 passes through the forest as far as Montfort-l'Amaury where the Bretons of Paris hold a procession every year.

The path now runs by the Butte de Neauphlé-le-Château and the Parc de l'Ecole Nationale d'Agriculture before passing the Parc de Wideville where there is a *nymphée*, a small Italianate grotto built around a spring. Finally, a few kilometres further on, we are back to Feucherolles and the fascinating 600 kilometre circuit of the GR1 is complete.

IDEAS FOR WALKS

ONE DAY WALKS
between stations or bus-stops

Porte-Maillot to Marnes-la-Coquette	13Km
Marnes-la-Coquette to Saint-Nom-la-Bretèche	16Km
Saint-Nom-la-Bretèche to Vernouillet-Verneuil	25Km
Triel-sur-Seine to Us	23Km
Santeuil to Pontoise	26Km
Pontoise to L'Isle-Adam	23Km
L'Isle-Adam to Viarmes	24Km
Viarmes to Orry-la-Ville-Coye	15Km
Orry-la-Ville to Ermenonville	25Km
Ermenonville to Dammartin-Juilly-Saint-Mard	20Km
Dammartin-Juilly-Saint-Mard to Meaux	22Km
Meaux to Crécy-la-Chapelle	16.5Km
Crécy-la-Chapelle to Marles-en-Brie	22Km
Marles-en-Brie to Verneuil-l'Etang	17Km
Verneuil-l'Etang to Melun	34Km
Melun to Fontainebleau-Avon	24Km
Boigneville to Boutigny-sur-Essonne	22Km
Boutigny-sur-Essonne to Lardy	24Km
Lardy to Saint-Chéron	22Km
Saint-Chéron to Dourdan	16Km
Dourdan to Rambouillet	31Km
(Same section by the PR)	23Km
Rambouillet to Le Perray	23Km
Méré-Montfort-l'Amaury to Feucherolles (bus)	22Km
Feucherolles (bus) to Saint-Nom-de-la-Bretèche	18Km
Feucherolles (bus) to Saint-Germain-en-Laye	20Km
Saint-Germain-en-Laye to Achères-Ville	15Km
Viarmes to Précy-sur-Oise	18Km
Boran to Saint-Leu-d'Esserent	20Km
Isles-Armentières to Meaux	23Km
Le Perray to Coignières	22Km

TWO DAY WALKS

Day 1	Auvers-sur-Oise to L'Isle-Adam	14Km
Day 2	L'Isle-Adam to Viarmes	24Km
Day 1	L'Isle-Adam to Viarmes	24Km
Day 2	Viarmes to Orry-la-Ville	15Km
Day 1	Orry-la-Ville to Ermenonville	25Km
Day 2	Ermenonville to Dammartin-Juilly-Saint-Mard	20Km
Day 1	Dourdan to the Maison Forestière des Hauts-Besnèires	23Km
Day 2	Maison Forestière des Hauts-Besnières to Rambouillet	13Km

Walks of 3, 4 and 5 days or more can be done by combining some of the one or two day routes.

The times indicated in the guide are for a non-stop walking pace of 4km per hour.

Echelle 1:25 000
1 cm pour 250 m

WALK 1

La Porte Maillot

The GR1 leaves Paris itself from the central reservation of the main crossroads at La Porte Maillot (reached by Metro Line 1, Line C of the RER and several buses).

In the Bois de Boulogne, a royal forest converted into a park by Napoleon III, there are rare trees and interesting landscapes to see.

The red-and-white waymarkers are few and far between in the section from A to G.

Begin by following the yellow waymarkers of the connecting route between the Metro station and the Bois. Take the subway to the south of the central reservation and turn right onto the Boulevard Périphérique when you come out. Upon entering the Bois de Boulogne, follow the path which leaves the main avenue until you come to the Ruisseau d'Armenonville. Cross the stream and you will find point A at the junction with the GR de Pays. This is a so-called *itinéraire du pourtour* with yellow-and-red waymarkers.

7Km
1:45

Take the 'Diagonale des Ruisseaux', a path with yellow-and-blue waymarkers which follows the right bank of the stream to the Route de l'Etoile and then the left bank to Longchamp.
At point P (yellow connecting path coming from the left), the man-made stream from the lake joins the Ruisseau d'Armenonville which flows north and the Ruisseau de Longchamp which flows south. After point Q, follow the Ruisseau de Longchamp for 1.8 kilometres to point R.
On the left, opposite the Lac Réservoir de la Grande Cascade, there is a junction with the yellow connecting path. Head towards the knoll and go down to the lake. Follow the underground drainage channel through the artificial rock and come out next to a cedar of Lebanon. Beyond the Chalet Restaurant de la

Grande Cascade, there is a road leading to point G.

Turn right and skirt Longchamp racecourse. Pass below the mill and then cut off towards the Seine via the Etang de Suresnes and the Carrefour des Tribunes. Go down onto the bank and follow it for 1.2 kilometres until you come to the outer limit of the city of Paris at a place called the 'Grille de Saint-Cloud'.
Cross the Seine and the railway line by the Passerelle de l'Avre and then proceed up the Rue A. Moguez.
Take the Rue du Mont-Valérien on the left and then follow the Rue Armengaud until you come to the Gare de Saint-Cloud.

SAINT-CLOUD

The Parc de Saint-Cloud covers some 392 hectares. Part of it is closed at night. Don't miss magnificent 17th-century fountain: the 37m jet operates on Sundays June to September; in mid-May and mid-September, the fountain is switched off because of visiting fun-fairs. An interesting history museum at the entrance.

1.5Km
0:20

Go through the subway. Outside, turn right onto the Rue Dailly and then continue along the Rue Hébert. Turn right onto the Avenue de Paris and then left onto the Avenue du Parc. Enter the Parc de Saint-Cloud through the Grille des Ecoles.

Turn right onto the Allée de Retz and gradually slant off to the left, skirting the Jardin du Trocadero. On reaching the Rond Point des Vingt-Quatre Jets, turn off diagonally right and follow the edge of the Bassin du Fer-à-Cheval. Turn right onto the Allée du Fer-à-Cheval.

Fer-à-Cheval

Detour *30 mins from Pont de Saint-Cloud (Metro Line 10).*

1Km
0:15

Detour see left. Enter the park by the Porte Clemenceau and go down the steps to the Place Clemenceau. For 300 metres, follow the railings on the left beside the N187. Turn right after coming to the waterfall. Cross the Grande Allée and turn left in front of the large fountain. Turn left into the Allée de Tranche-Montagne, which brings you onto the broad Allée du Mail. When you come to the end, turn left in order to rejoin the Fer-à-Cheval.

The GR1 now follows the Allée de la Balustrade to a roundabout of the same name. Carry on to the right and this will bring you down into La Butte-aux-Chèvres.

La Butte-aux-Chèvres

Detour 20 mins
from Sèvres (Metro Line 9).

Detour see left. Come out of the Pont-de-Sèvres Metro station on the Boulogne side and cross the bridge. Now take the footbridge which leads to Parc de Saint-Cloud. As soon as you enter the gate, turn left and continue until you come to the Allée Verte, which is beyond the pitch for boules. This will bring you to a bridge above the Porte du Mail. Turn right and then left a few metres before reaching a zig-zag road rising steeply to La Butte-aux-Chèvres.

Head towards a wooden fence and then keep it on your right until you come to the end. Now, beyond the enclosure, leave the metalled road and take the path leading into the woods. Follow the park wall until you go through the Ville-d'Avray gate. Cross the Rond Carré and the N185. Keep to the right of the Pelouse de la Brosse and carry on up into the woods.

3Km
0:45

At the top, turn right and then left. Cross a roundabout and turn right into a road leading to La Porte Blanche.

Detour 10 mins
from the Gare de Garches.

Detour see left. On leaving the station, turn left and pass over the level crossing. Cross the autoroute and enter the Parc de Saint-Cloud. Take the first tarmac road to the right. As soon as you come into Marnes-la-Coquette through La Porte Blanche, follow the GR. It goes straight towards Marly via Marnes-la-Coquette, turning left towards the Pont de Saint-Cloud or the Pont de Sèvres via the Parc de Saint-Cloud.

Pass through the Porte Blanche to enter Marnes-la-Coquette.

MARNES-LA-COQUETTE

When you come to the square, pass by the church on your left and follow the Rue George-et-Xavier-Schlumberger.

Junction with the PR de Fausses-Reposes.

At the traffic light, turn right into the Rue Yves-Carrière (N407) and carry on to the second bend. Turn off to the left on a road going up

25

through the Bois de Marnes.

At the junction with the third avenue, at the corner of lots 40 and 43, leave the yellow waymarkers of the PR de Fausses-Reposes diagonally on your left. Continue along the edge of the Bois de Marnes, paying close attention to the waymarkers. This will bring you out onto a road alongside the A13 autoroute. Follow the road for a few metres until you come to the D182. Turn right and cross the autoroute at a major junction. Carry straight on along the Boulevard de Jardy. Turn right onto the Avenue du Bois and then left onto the Avenue des Terrasses. When you come to the traffic lights, cross the Boulevard de Jardy and follow the Rue Allouard until you reach the Gare de Vaucresson.

3Km
0:45

VAUCRESSON

⌂ ✕ ♈ ⚏ ⛟ ▭

Junction with the GR de Pays de la Ceinture Verte coming from Rueil.

The GR de Pays de la Ceinture Verte branches off towards Chaville.

Take the subway under the Avenue de la République. Go left and follow the railway line until you turn off left again on the path of the Bois des Dames. Turn left yet again onto the Route des Puits (D173) and cross the junction.

2Km
0:30

Enter the woods along an avenue with a north north-west orientation. Pass in front of the Pavillon du Butard and then turn left onto a track which descends through the Bois de la Celle. Cross the D128E and continue on the Avenue Gustave-Mesureur which is directly opposite. At the end, cross the junction and take the Sente des Bérangères on the left. At the end of this path, on the left, you come to the Gare de Bougival.

BOUGIVAL

⌂ ✕ ♈ ⚏ ⛟ ▭

Detour *10 mins*
from the station, turn right onto the Sente de la Station and then onto the Avenue de Lyautey.

Turn left on the Avenue de Lyautey and go under the railway bridge. Turn first left and then right to take the Grande-Rue to the woods. When you come to the second entrance of the Propriété Le Camp, turn right. Keeping the orchards on your left, take two turnings to the left.

3Km
0:45

At the other end of the Propriété Le Camp, take the road going off to the right.
On the right, the tomb of Maréchal Joffre is to be found on a private property (Louveciennes). The initial J above crossed field marshal's batons is to be seen above the main gate.

A turn to the left will now bring you back to the N186. Cross the road, turn left and carry on for about 150 metres until you come to the Maison Forestière des Deux-Portes.

Maison Forestière des Deux-Portes

This marks the entrance to the state forest of Marly (2,254 hectares); fine woods of oak, chestnut and birch. Before the forest lies the Parc de Marly, formerly the grounds of the château built by Louis XIV. The GR1 runs through the forest to the Tapis-Vert. The names of all the avenues through the forest are given in the 1:25,000 map of the Forêts de l'Ouest de l'Île-de-France No. 419.

3Km
0:45

To the right, there is a fine view of the Parc de Marly as far as the Grille Royale. The rectangle that can be seen below is the site of the former royal château.

Take the Route des Deux-Portes along the edge of the Réservoirs de Marly. After a right-hand bend, take the path through the trees till you come to a metalled road. Cross the road and go down into the valley. When you come up on the other side, turn left and this will bring you to the Rond-point du Tapis-Vert, from where there is a view over the Parc de Marly.

Follow the road to the right for 100 metres and then turn left. Near to another road, turn right onto a forest track for a few metres. Now turn left into an avenue and follow it to a crossroads.

Go diagonally to the left, paying close attention to the waymarkers, until you reach the forest wall. Turn left and follow the wall, first along a gravel track and then a tarmac road. On the right, you will soon come to the junction with the Marly-le-Roi detour.

GARE DE MARLY-LE-ROI DETOUR

🏠 🍴 🍷 🚉 🚌 🚃

Detour *30 mins from the Gare de Marly.*

Detour see left. When you come out of the station, follow the Avenue du Général Leclerc. At the crossroads, take the Rue A. Dumas and then the Rue de l'Eglise. When you reach the Eglise Saint-Vigor, turn right onto the Route de Saint-Cyr which immediately bends left. After 500 metres, turn left on a forest path which leads to the GR1.

4Km
1:00

Marly is a picturesque old town. Of Louis XIV's château, nothing now remains but the memory and the park, through which the GR1 passes. See the 17th-century church and the drinking trough.

On the last bend in the road, take a short cut leading to the D7. Cross this road and turn left on the parallel forest track which will bring you to the viewpoint of the Val de Cruye. Turn right and go down into the Val de Cruye as far as the roundabout of the Etoile Bizarre. Cross the D161 and continue until you come into a corrie basin called Le Saladier. Make your way through the bracken and climb out of the hollow on the opposite side.

When you get to Beau Vallon, take the road on the right, running more or less parallel to the Route Royale. Turn right into the Route Levreau which brings you to the start of the Saint-Nom-la-Bretèche detour.

Saint-Nom-la-Bretèche detour
Detour *20 mins from the station.*

Detour see left. Go up the road and over the railway bridge. Turn right onto the road that follows the railway line and then leave it almost immediately to take a road branching off to the left. When you come to a crossroads, take the rutted track on the left to join the GR1.

2.5Km
0:40

Follow the Route Levreau. Turn right onto the Route de la Croix-Saint-Michel and follow it until you come to the cross and panoramic viewpoint. Now turn left and cross the D98. Take the road that leads to the Carrefour du Renard and then the forest track that cuts the Route Dauphine. Shortly afterwards, turn left and cross the Route des Princesses. Directly in front of you is the Route des Chasseurs, which you follow to the Etoile des Chasseurs.

Etoile des Chasseurs

On the right, there is a branch of the GR1 which leads to the Forêt de Saint-Germain and to Achères.Go west towards Meulan until you come to the Route Dauphine.

Turn right into an avenue which runs in a north-westerly direction across two valleys. The route now passes under the A13. Follow the road for a few metres and then turn right onto a path leading to a crossroads.

5.5Km
1:30

Turn right (north-east) and then left (north). Paying close attention to the waymarkers, follow the path to the bottom of the valley. Climb up the other side almost as far as the road (Carrefour du Précipice). Turn right and go down the track for riders. Turn left onto a path which follows a tumbledown wall. At the Etoile du Silence, take the road on your right and follow it to Sainte-Gemme.

SAINTE-GEMME

1.5Km
0:20

Go south through the town, turning diagonally right (south-west) near a chapel. Cross the D30 and continue until you come to a crossroads.

Crossroads

The crossroads lies to the north of Feucherolles and marks the junction of the southern branch of the GR1 coming from the Forêt de Rambouillet and Montfort-l'Amaury.

6.5Km
1:40

MONTAMETS
✕ 🚊 🚌

0.5Km
0:10

Junction with the GR26

At this crossroads, you will see the platform of a former tramway line. This once formed part of a large suburban railway network which allowed market gardeners to deliver their produce to Les Halles in Paris.

4Km
1:00

Marsinval

3Km
0:45

Turn right and proceed first north and then north-west. Cross the D30 bypass and reach the Croix Sainte-Geneviève. Turn right. Cross a road and pass between the Ferme des Beurreries and the radio station. Follow the track on the left until you come to the Route des Flambertins d'Orgeval. Turn right and follow the route for 700 metres. Now turn left onto a track which brings you to the Bois de la Garenne and continues, skirting the woods. Take the Rue des Bouillons until you come to the Moulin d'Orgeval.

Follow the Route de la Verte-Salle. Turn off to the left on a track which climbs up between the orchards. Cross the D45 and go down the other side along the Route de la Vente-Bertine till you come to Montamets.

Go north out of the village and, where the road bends right, take a track leading to the junction with the GR26.

Continue north, crossing the D113 and passing under the A13 autoroute.

Before the church at Bures, turn right and follow the 'Val Joli' (château). Now turn left into a lane which leads north-east, continuing as a grassy path which brings you to a crossroads. Go directly across and take the Chemin de Brezolles. At the top of the rise, turn right. Where you come out of the woods, there is a view over the hills of L'Hautil. Turn left here onto the road through the old village of Marsinval.

Go north-east along a track through the orchards and then turn left onto a road leading north. Branch off to the right and follow the dirt track which runs north-east parallel to the Vallée Goujon. Leave the track before the high voltage line and turn left on the Sente des Poiriers. This takes you north-west, passing under electricity cables. (Care is needed as there are no waymarkers on this section.) You now pass in front of the church of Vernouillet.

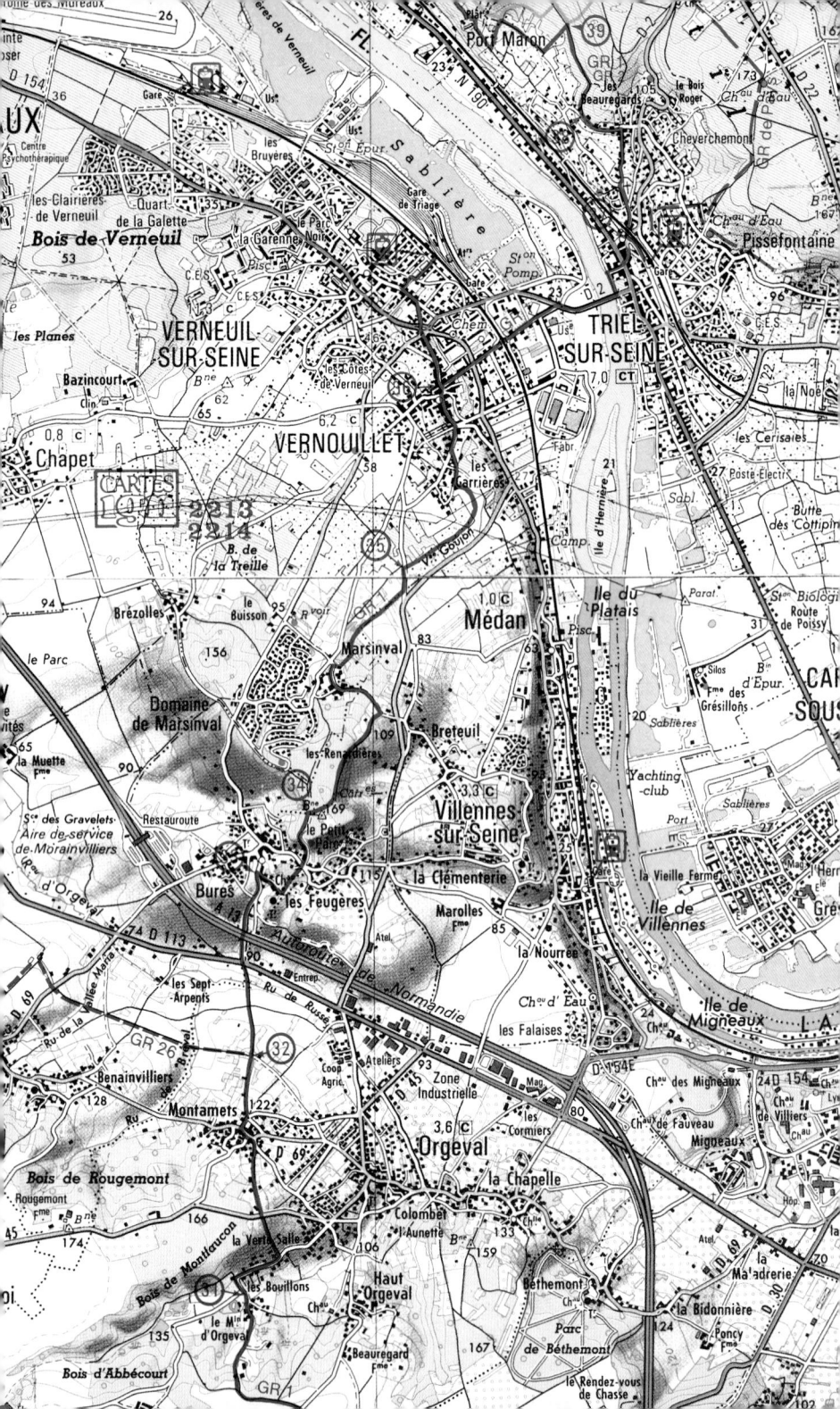

VERNOUILLET

🏠 🍴 🍷 ⛴ 🚌

Notice the bell tower. This is the finest of the 17 churches of Agnès de Montfort, Comtesse de Meulan.

2Km
0:30

Detour *15 mins*
from the station.
Follow the detour waymarkers (white and red with white stripes).

TRIEL-SUR-SEINE

🏠 🍴 🍷 ⛴ 🚌 🚆

Worth visiting the church, a blend of Gothic and Renaissance styles. Notice the 12th-century façade, the 16th-century south doorway, Renaissance chancel over the Rue Galande and the 16th-century stained glass windows by Jean le Prince.

6Km
1:30

D14E2

Detour *20 mins*
from the Gare de Vaux-sur-Seine.

2Km
0:30

Turn right outside the station. Cross the bridge and go up on the other side, taking the second turning on the right.

EVECQUEMONT

🍴

Turn right onto the Rue Jean-Jaurès. Cross the Boulevard de l'Europe (D154) and join the road to the Pont de la Seine. Cross the bridge and follow the slope down to the right. The GR1 passes along the embankment and through picturesque streets before joining the Rue de l'Hautil.

The GR1 and the GR2 follow the same route as far as La Marèche.

Go under the bridge and then turn right up the Rue Galande. Turn off to the left on the Rue des Bois and then right just after the cemetery. At the junction, turn left into the Grande Sente des Beaux-Regards. At the top of a slope, take the right-hand track which forks down through the undergrowth. Continue down to the left until you turn right onto a gravelled road. After following the edge of the fields for some distance, you come to a downhill stretch. Here, at a place called Port Maron, turn right onto another track and along a sort of esplanade with a view of the Seine. Continue straight on until you come to a fork.

Ignore the Rue du Bel-Air which goes off to the left and continue straight ahead. Now climb up to the right along the Chemin des Petites-Carrières. Go through a small wood and then follow the road down towards Vaux-sur-Seine. Turn right and take the Rue du Temple up to the plateau at a point called Le Jonquet. Now bear to the right to reach the D14E2.

Cross the D14E2 and pass the Château de Fort-Vache on your left. Continue straight on and across a road. In a small wood, take the left-hand fork to come to the first houses of Evecquemont.

Go all the way through the village and out the other side. As the road climbs up and bends

2Km
0:30

JUNCTION
of the GR1 and GR2
🏠 ✕ ♉ ⚖ 🚌
Detour *50 mins*
from the Gare de Meulan.

4Km
1:00

left, turn off to the right on a short steep slope. Cross the D922 and continue straight ahead through fields and orchards. At a point where the track begins to descend to the right and within sight of a half-buried water tower, look for the opening of another track going off to the left. Follow this down to the junction with the Meulan detour.

Detour see left. Go left down the Avenue de la Gare, turning off left onto the Boulevard Carnot and then the Rue Georges-Clemenceau. Go up the Rue de la Chaîne and turn left into La Côte Saint-Nicholas. When you reach the church, go left down the steps at its eastern end and then follow the Ruelle Sainte-Avoie. Next, turn left and go down as far as the Rue des Carrières. Turn right and go up the Impasse des Réservoirs. Turn left and continue to the end of the cemetery where you go down to the left over waste ground. At the bottom, turn off to the right through bushes until you come to a housing estate. Go down to the left along the Allée de l'Ibis and the Allée de l'Île-de-France till you come to a crossroads. From here, take the little private road going north-east. Go through the subway under the D922 and then continue on the road to the north-east. Where the road forks, take the gravelled road on the right to the junction with the GR1 and GR2.

At this point, the GR2 carries straight on towards Vernon.

The GR1 turns right onto the gravelled road towards La Marêche. Just before you reach a long stone wall, turn off to the left by a transformer and go down the steep slope. In the village square at Villette, bear left and then turn right onto the Rue des Champs. Cut across the D28 and go up along the edge of the conifers. Particular care must now be taken as there are no waymarkers.

Shortly before the road passes between two hedgerows, turn right onto a track between the fields, leading towards a barn. The GR comes

35

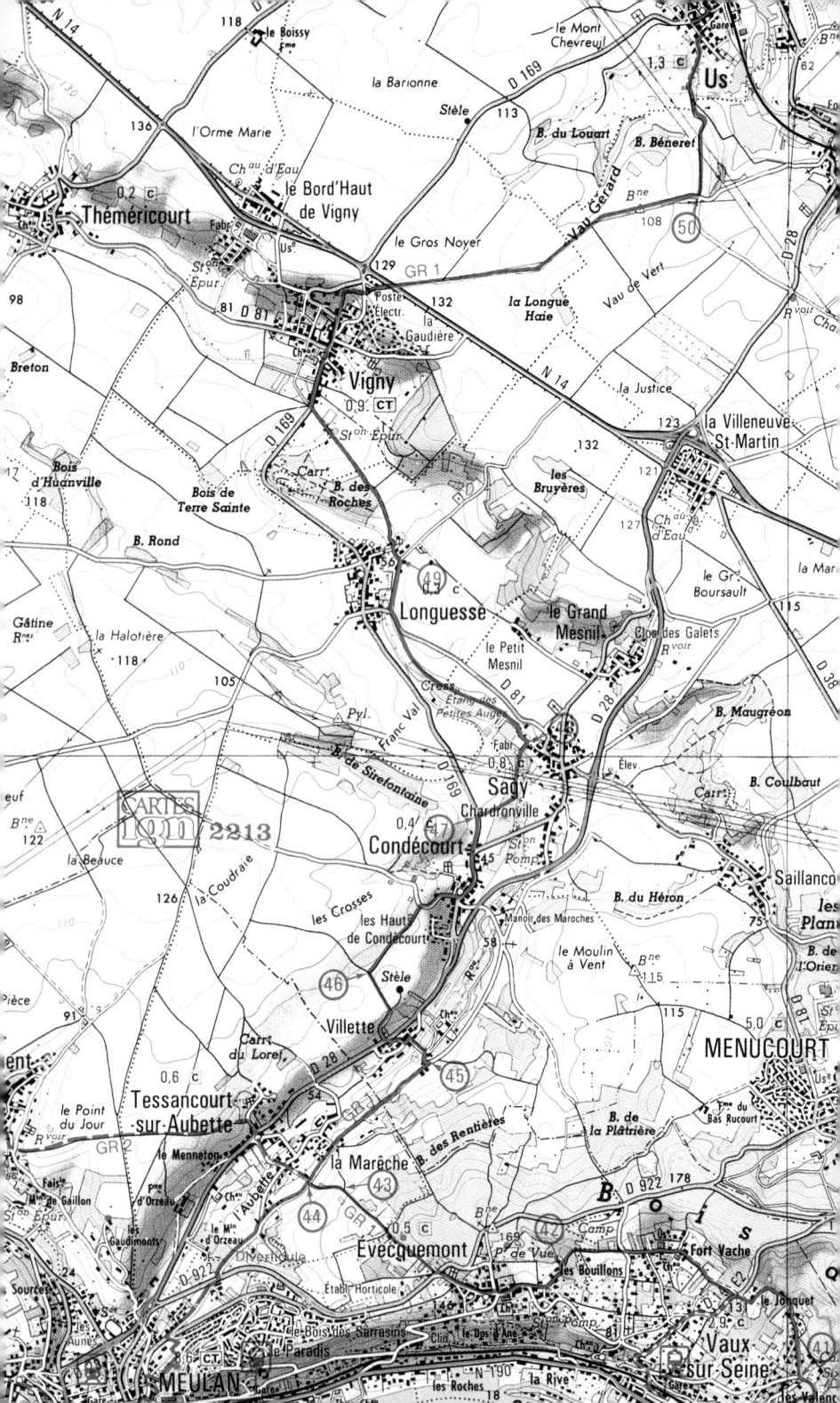

onto a minor road towards Condécourt. Pass below the church and take the D169 in the direction of Vigny. Turn off the road onto the first track to the right. Now turn left and follow a grassy lane along the edge of a wood. This brings you to a sports field on the outskirts of Sagy.

SAGY

The GR does not go into the village but the old houses, lovely farms and solid church make it worth a short detour (to the right).

4Km
1:00

Turn left and continue past the stadium until you reach the junction on the way into Longuesse. Do not bear left into the centre of the village but continue straight ahead on the Chemin du Marais. Turn left off the tarmac road onto a grassy path.

Pick up the road again just before the bend and go up the gravelled track which is directly in front. When you reach the gate to the grounds of a château, turn right onto the Rue de la Comté which brings you to Vigny.

VIGNY

The very fine château, built under Louis XII, is closed to the public but can be seen from the grounds (entry charge, picnicking permitted).

5Km
1:15

The GR continues along the Rue du Général Leclerc before climbing a grassy lane. Go under the N14 and then diagonally out to the right on a good track. Careful attention must now be paid to the instructions as there are no waymarkers. Just after the beginning of a downhill stretch, there is a junction with a road coming from the right. Turn left onto a track with views over the valley of the Viosne before descending into Us.

US

Detour *5 mins from the station.*
Bear left to go over the level crossing and then up a road heading slightly left until you come to the east end of the church.

3.5Km
1:00

The GR turns left into the Rue de la Villeneuve-Saint-Martin and then right into the Rue Jean-Jaurès before reaching the church.

The GR goes round the church and continues along the Rue Henri-Clément. At the next junction, take the Rue de Dampont. The Château de Dampont can be seen clearly on the other side of the valley. At the next junction, turn right on a road which takes you over the railway line and then over the River Viosne. At Dampont, turn left into the Vallée d'Orémus and then up onto the plateau. This brings you to a path which marks the junction with the Santeuil-Le Perchay detour.

Detour *1hr*
Santeuil and Le Perchay

Detour see left. To get from the GR1 to the Gare de Santeuil (15 minutes), turn left onto

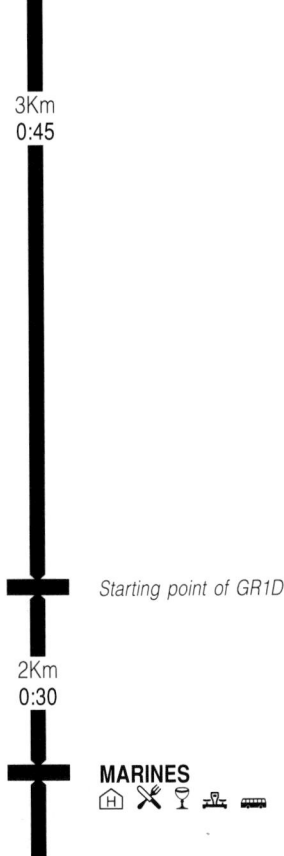

3Km
0:45

Starting point of GR1D

2Km
0:30

MARINES

7Km
1:45

the road into Santeuil (café – restaurant). Take the first turning on the left at a junction dominated by the church with its 12th-century tower. Turn left and follow the Rue Jean-Mermoz. Cross the Viosne and you now come to the Gare de Santeuil. To continue to the gîte d'étape at Le Perchay (45 minutes) follow the D51 past the ru la Couleuvre and then take the Route du Perchay which is directly in front. Turn left onto a track parallel to the Route d'Us and continue up the Vallée aux Moines.

Come into Perchay along the Rue du Cornouiller. When you come to a small square, turn right on the Grande-Rue which takes you out of the village. The gîte d'étape is on the left.

The GR1 now heads east to a road junction near a wood.

Bear off to the north-west, crossing a road and following the side of a sports field before reaching the junction of the D159 and the D51. Turn right onto the D51 in the direction of Marines and continue until you come to a bend where there are two disused reservoirs.

Take the straight road ahead of you and then turn right towards Marines which is clearly visible from a good distance. Bear slightly to the right after a large scrapyard and then follow the edge of the cemetery. The GR1 now takes the Rue du Goulet into Marines.

Cross the D915 and make your way to the Place de Verdun via the Rue J.B. Cartry and the Rue du Docteur-Meynard. After turning left into the Rue Malebranche, the GR comes to the Place Dubois-Danger and continues straight ahead along a little street for pedestrians only. Turn left into the Rue A. Baleydier before leaving Marines on the Rue du Boeuf.

At the junction of several tracks, before you come to a wood, turn right into a sunken lane which brings you out into a field. The lane skirts a wood for a while before going through it and then on to Bréançon. Go through the village along the Rue de la Liberté and the Rue

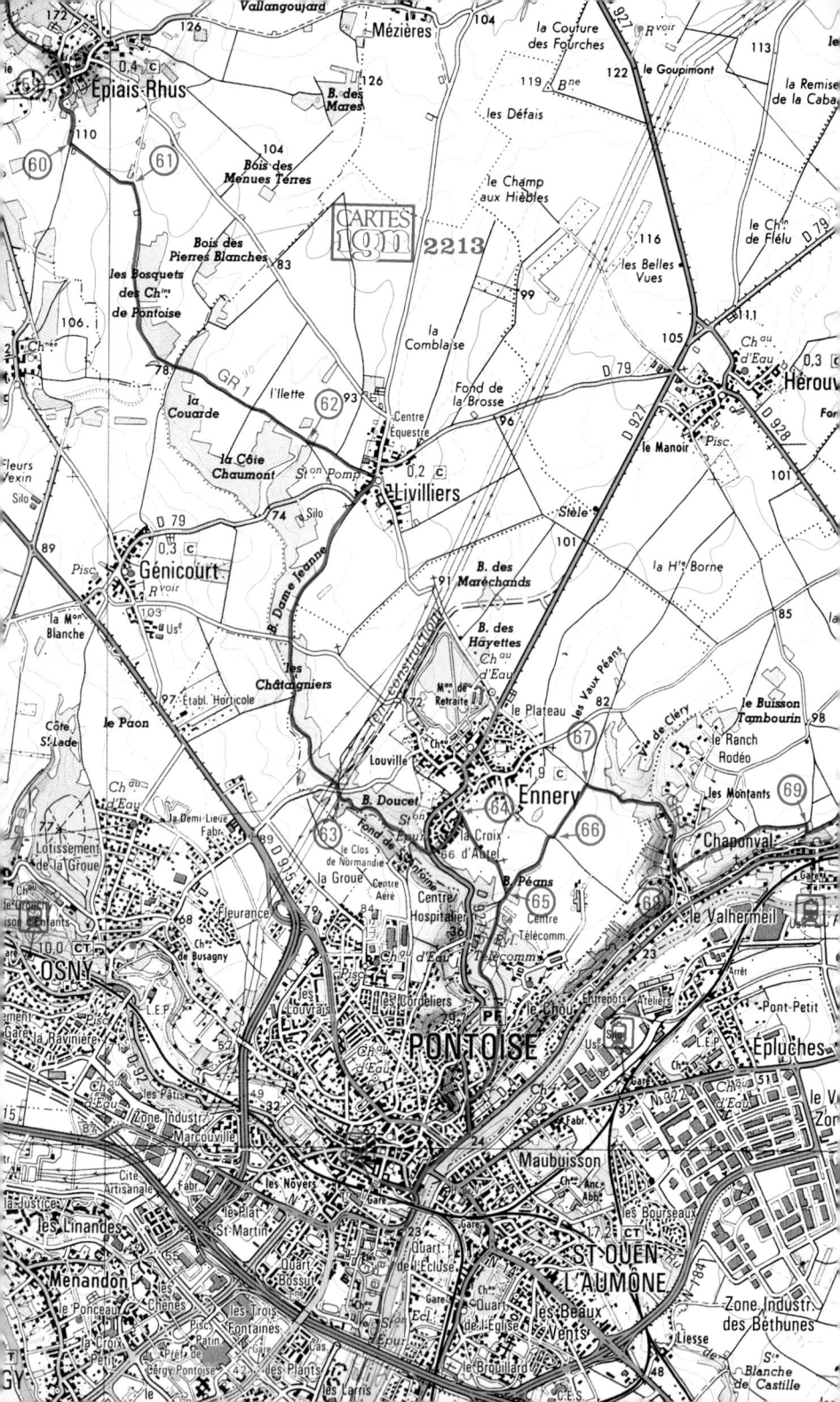

de l'Eglise. After leaving Bréançon, continue along the D64 till you come to the bottom of a hill. Turn off on the second dirt track to the left, opposite a disused station. Thanks to the owner's permission, the GR continues through the former railway cutting and then along a tree-lined gravel road. Branch off to the right near a wood and follow the lower side of the cutting. Turn left onto a road.

Turn right onto a gravel road leading to Grisy-les-Plâtres.

GRISY-LES-PLÂTRES

Turn left by the cross near the first houses into the Rue de l'Isle and then take the first turning on the right into the Rue de Berval. Turn left again onto the D64 which will bring you into the Place de l'Eglise from the right. Bear left and pass the post office on the Rue Robert Machy. At the end of this road, turn left into the Rue du Butel and then immediately right into a lane between hedges and houses.
There are good views along the path which brings you into Epiais-Rhus (expensive restaurant and little cafe) via the Chemin du Butard. Turn right down the Rue des Bruyères and pass a fine dovecote on the right. The road continues after a junction as the Ruelle de Vanne.

6Km
1:30

A brief detour to the left will take you to the small square where there is a church with a fine tower. The GR goes down a wide dirt track. Turn left off the track. Bear right, away from the copse on your left, and head towards a barn and wood.

Warning In the reverse direction, there may be no waymarkers at this junction.

The GR follows the edge of the wood and then veers away to the left. The route now goes straight across fields, passing through two small woods. As you enter the second wood, take the left fork which will bring you to Livilliers.

LIVILLIERS

Just before the church, turn right on the Route de Génicourt. By a cross where the road leaves the village, move onto a dirt track.

4.5Km
1:00

Continue in the same direction, first across fields and then along the edge of the Bois de la Dame-Jeanne. Cross a minor road and descend into a wooded valley. This brings you out at the edge of the woods onto a better track which bends slightly to the left. Pass under one road and across another. Then turn left into a sunken lane in the Bois Doucet. This bends left into the first track upwards. The track veers off immediately to the right, cutting across the D927 near the entrance to Ennery.

Detour

Interesting church dating from 12th and 16th centuries. Château. Cafe-restaurant and bakery.

Go up between two small buildings and continue in the same direction along the Rue du Chêne through a housing estate. Turn off to the right on a track across the fields. Near an isolated cross, bear right and go down to the bottom of a valley. This will bring you to the edge of the Bois Péans.

BOIS PÉANS

Junction with the GR de Pays de la Ceinture Verte which leads off to the right towards Pontoise.

Detour *45 mins from the station by the GR de Pays.*

Detour see left. Cross the Place du Général-de-Gaulle and continue directly up the Rue Thiers before turning right into the Rue Pierre-Butin. At a bend in the road, take the path opposite, the Ruelle de la Croix-du-Bourg and

---

Pontoise

Built like an amphitheatre, Pontoise is an ancient town and former fortress. In the Middle Ages, its strategic position at the confluence of the Oise and the Viosne made it one of the keys to the Vexin.

Visit Saint-Maclou cathedral built between the 12th and 16th centuries; the panoramic view of the château grounds; the church of Notre Dame; the museums; the Gothic cellars and underground port.

At the end of the 19th century, Pontoise was much favoured by painters of the Impressionist school. Pisarro lived in the Rue de l'Hermitage and Cézanne went there to paint. Legend has it that many Impressionist canvases are still jealously kept by old families in the town. To the south-west, the new town of Cergy-Pontoise is being built in the valley of the Oise between Pontoise and Conflans Sainte-Honorine. It is being constructed in a horse-shoe shape on the heights overlooking the Oise. The central area is defined by the Neuville meander, which is being kept as a recreation area with facilities for many sports and a natural park around the lakes.

then the Rue du Château (Pisarro Museum and château grounds, panoramic views over Pontoise, the Oise and Saint-Ouen-l'Aumône). Turn right in the Rue de la Roche and come out in the Place du Pont. Instead of crossing the river, continue along the right bank on the Quai du Pothuis.

Go past the Route de Dieppe (Boulevard Jean-Jaurès). Turn left into the Rue de l'Hermitage (D927) and then, at the first traffic light, turn right into the steeply rising Rue Adrien-Lemoine (cave dwellings on the left). At the top of the hill, take the right-hand fork, which is the Chemin du Bois-Péans. When you come to the last house on the left, level with the corner of a long concrete wall, turn left onto a path which winds along the edge of the old quarries (views over Pontoise). The path becomes wider and now leads you all the way through the Bois Péans. When you come out of the wood, cross the road and take the dirt track opposite. After a short distance, turn right and join the GR1 just before entering the wood.

6Km
1:30

Coming from Ennery, the GR1 turns left into the Bois Péans. When it comes out on the other side, there are no waymarkers for 1 kilometre so careful attention must be paid to the description and map. Carry on straight ahead on a plateau between two fields.

Turn right onto a dirt track, coming from Ennery which can be seen away to the left. You now return to the original heading (north north-east) and come to a crossroads. Turn right and follow the faint path between two fields till you come to the edge of a wood. Bear right and follow the edge of the wood along an ill-defined track. After about 100 metres, turn left onto a well-marked stretch which brings you to a sunken lane. Go downhill under the trees until you come to a tarmac road. Turn left and continue until you come to the edge of Valhermeil. Take the minor road to the right.

Turn left onto the Sente des Jardins. The way is tarmacadamed at the beginning but soon turns into a steep path climbing to the left. Ignore two small paths going off to the right.

After crossing the plateau, the GR descends towards the first houses of Chaponval.

The path immediately climbs back to the edge of the plateau and then, shortly afterwards, descends along a sunken lane through trees, coming close to the first houses of Auvers. The GR now turns 90° left into a narrow sunken lane and returns to the plateau. Follow to the right an electricity line carried on concrete posts. This brings you past an iron cross and into a wood. Cross a road and continue directly along a dirt road on the plateau. The GR now comes to gardens and a few houses. High banks rise on either side until the GR comes out onto a road. Go left here and shortly afterwards turn right down the D928 for about 200 metres. At the first junction, turn left. ' The road now goes under a stone bridge and brings you to a cross surrounded by trees in the heart of Auvers-sur-Oise.

AUVERS-SUR-OISE

The local tourist board has set up a picnic area for walkers.
Charming spot with its terraces rising above the right bank of the Oise. Its scenery has been the inspiration of many artists, including Daubigny and Vincent Van Gogh. It was here that Van Gogh met his dramatic end and was buried alongside his brother Theo. See the 12th-and 13th-century church.
Detour *10 mins from the station (yellow-and-red waymarkers).*

5Km
1:30

Detour see left. Outside the station, turn left on the D928. After the hôtel de ville, turn right onto the Rue de la Sansonne and go past the tourist office. Turn left into the Rue Daubigny where you will find the GR waymarker in a leafy square.

Turn left out of the square on the Rue Daubigny. Where the road forks, bear left and continue into the Bois Le Roi. Go all the way through the wood and then along the edge in

45

the Ravine des Vallées. Turn right onto a minor road and continue till you come to a junction with a cross on the right and a transformer on the left. Carry straight on along the dirt road in more or less the same direction. When you enter the wood, the road descends very steeply. Cross the road from Nesles-la-Vallée to Valmondois.

According to tradition, La Fontaine is supposed to have written the fable of the Miller, his Son and the Ass at the Mill of Burgaud in Valmondois.

Continue straight ahead until you come to the disused local railway station at La Nase.

La Nase
Detour *45 mins*
from the Gare de Valmondois
(yellow waymarkers of the PR circuit).

Detour see left. Head towards Valmondois along the Avenue de la Gare. After the car park, take the Rue des Violaines. At a bend, turn off into the Rue de la Division-Leclerc which is almost opposite. Where the railway line belonging to the transport museum of the Vallée du Sausseron crosses the road, turn right and follow the railway track. The path then continues between the River Sausseron and the D151 to La Nase.

4Km
1:00

Turn off to the left on the old road and follow it to Nesles-la-Vallée, crossing the D151 and the D79. When you reach the D64, just before the disused Gare de Nesles, turn right and cross the Sausseron. Continue along the D64/D151.

NESLES-LA-VALLÉE
12th-and 13th-century church.

At the crossroads beyond the River Sausseron, turn right towards the church and follow the D151 for about 1 kilometre.
Where the road bends right, turn off on a minor road which forks to the left. After crossing a stream, the road becomes a track and it is essential to follow the waymarkers closely.

5Km
1:30

You now emerge from bushes into a field. Turn right and follow the hedge to the wood. When you come out of the wood, turn right. At the last clump of trees, bear right and cross the plateau. Go down first by a minor road and then the D4. Take the first road on the left and this will bring you to the Gare de Parmain -

L'ISLE-ADAM

🏠 ⌂ 🅰 🍴 🍷 🚂 🚐

The town gets its name from Seigneur de Villiers, who, in 1104, built a castle on the Île de l'Oise and a priory on the river bank. The estate of the De Villiers family passed into the hands of the Montmorencys and then into those of the Bourbon-Conti. Visit the 16th-century church (doorway and pulpit), museum and, on the island, the terrace, which is all that remains of the Conti château.

7Km
1:40

Detour *30 mins*
gîte d'étape.

Île de Champagne

On the Île de la Cohue, go left and take the footbridge over to the left bank of the Oise. Continue north to the Île de Champagne.

Carrefour Vicaire

Detour *3 hrs*
from Taverny.

Aux Sapins Brûlés is the junction with the GR de Pays de la Ceinture Verte de l'Île-de-France.

L'Isle-Adam. Go over the level crossing and then two bridges to reach the Île de la Cohue.

On the Île de la Cohue, go right and take the footbridge over to the left bank of the Oise. Follow the bank to the south until you come to the last houses. Turn left onto the D67. Leave the town and cross over the N322 into the Forêt de l'Isle-Adam. Immediately take the track along the wall, passing the Château de Vivray on the left. Turn left into the Route de Stors.

Turn into the first avenue on the right. At the end, turn left and follow the remains of a stone wall. Follow a narrow footpath and then a track to reach the Porte Noire. No trespassing on the nearby mushroom farms. Turn left onto the Route Neuve.Then turn right onto a footpath, which broadens out into an avenue and brings you up to the Carrefour Vicaire.

Detour see left. The waymarkers begin to the right of the Place de la Gare. Follow along a wall and across two streets. Carry straight on before turning off to the left on a path between two walls. Pass the entrance to the cemetery and go round the church. Follow the cemetery wall along a path rising up into the Forêt de Montmorency. A series of broad forest paths now takes you past a radar mast to Aux Sapins Brûlés.

Descend to the Route des Fonds. Cross the road and pass a pond on the left. About 100 metres further on, join the path going up to the Carrefour des Six Chiens. Bear right along the fence till you come to a crossroads. Turn right and, paying close attention to the waymarking, make your way to a place called Le Fay-en-Chauvry. Turn left onto a path which will bring you out onto the Route de Chauvry-Béthemont. Go left for about 20 metres and then turn right.

1.5Km
0:20

Take the D44 for a few metres (altitude marker 121) and then head directly north to the edge of the forest, still paying close attention to the waymarking. This brings you to the D9.

Go under the bridge of the N184. Make your way to the plateau up a zig-zag road as far as the edge of the forest. Once in the forest, turn left. Then bear first left and then right till you come to the Carrefour Vicaire.

Turn right into an avenue which takes you south-east to the Carrefour de la Porte Baillet. Go over the bridge on the N184 and then up in a north-easterly direction to the Carrefour du Poteau-de-la-Tour.

The GR1 takes a forest road in the same direction.

Turn left and pass in front of the Nerville water tower. At the edge of the forest, follow the fence of adjoining properties for about 500 metres. When you come to some ruins, turn left down a track through pastures and out onto the D64 at the entrance to Nerville-la-Forêt.

NERVILLE-LA-FORÉT

The GR comes into the village along the Rue Marcel-Harley. Continue along a road which leads to a track parallel to the N1. Cross over and turn right along the D64E for about 200 metres. Now take the N1 up to the junction with the Route de Presles. Take the unmarked road running between two tracks towards Presles. This brings you onto a small street at Ponthus. Turn right onto the Rue François-le-Cam and right again onto the Rue Pierre Brossolette (D78). After passing under the railway line, link up on the left with the Presles-Courcelles detour.

5Km
0:40

Detour
from the Gare de Presles
Turn left in the Place du
Général Leclerc and go over
the level crossing. Turn right
into the Rue Daniele-
Casanova and follow the
railway line.

1Km
0:15

Turn right and go along the D78 for 400 metres. Now go left on the gravel track leading to the ruined Moulin de Montbray. Cross the Rue de Presles and so come to Courcelles.

COURCELLES

X ♀ ⚶ ☕

7Km
1:45

The GR does not go through the town centre. At the junction of the Rue du Bois-Belle-Fille and the Rue Henry-Douay, bear diagonally to the right on the Rue de la Carrière to reach the Forêt de Carnelle. Turn left into the Route Germain Grue and then right into the Fond Champs Chiare. Cross the Route de la Pierre Turquaise and then go up through the wood to the site of the 'covered avenue' of La Pierre Turquaise. Go down to your left and follow the Route de la Pierre Turquaise for about 75 metres before turning off to the left.

Take the Route de la Touffe until you come to the junction of the Pas de Vache. Follow the right side of Lac Bleu and carry on from there to the second pool and then the Rue Gros Charme. Cross the D85. Turn left into the Route du Ringet and continue till you come to the Poteau du Carrefour de Carnelle. Turn right into the Route de la Touffe and then right again into the Route Tournante. Take the forest road on the left and come out at Noisy-sur-Oise.

NOISY-SUR-OISE

♀ ⚶ ▭▭▭

2Km
0:30

Go left on the Rue de Bossang and then turn left again into the Rue Jean-Jacques Rousseau. Now turn right successively on the Rue Pasteur, the Rue Paul-Bert and the Rue Jules-Ferry. From the Place Gambetta, take the Rue Victor Hugo and the Rue Georges-Marie Picot. Now cross through the meadows and fruit trees of the Clos des Champs to reach the entrance to Asnières-sur-Oise.

ASNIÈRES-SUR-OISE

X ♀ ⚶

Point of departure for the GR1A (see Walk 2, page 123)

2Km
0:45

Take the track on your right through vegetable gardens. Turn right onto a broad gravel track. Then turn left on the path leading to the Maison Forestière du Rond-Point de Chantilly. Cross the junction and go over a plateau before descending towards Viarmes. On the way down, turn right into the Chemin de la Fontaîne d'Amour (gîte d'étape). Go left along the Route de Viarmes at Saint-Martin-du-Tertre and then into Viarmes.

VIARMES

🏠 X ♀ ⚶

Church dating from the 12th, 15th and 16th centuries. The mairie is housed in an 18th-

Go along a tree-lined avenue and then cross the D909. Follow the Rue de la Gare to a fountain. Go left for 100 metres and then turn right into the Ruelle de la Nourrie. You now come to a road with villas on either side.

century château.

Detour *10 mins*
from the Gare de Viarmes.

3Km
0:45

SEUGY
🍸 🚉 🚂

3Km
0:45

LUZARCHES
🍴 🍸 🚉 🚂
Detour
from the station.
Cross the Place de la Gare
and go down the road
opposite. Go right along the
Rue du Pontcel to the
covered market.

Together, the two forests
cover some 1,650 hectares.
The first is almost entirely in
private hands but the other is

Detour see left. From the Place de la Gare, turn right along the Rue de la Justice. Go past a level crossing. The road eventually turns into a sunken lane, along which you continue as far as the Carrefour de la Rue des Champlâtreux.

Turn left into the Rue des Champlâtreux and go under the railway bridge. Turn left and follow a gravel track for about 50 metres. Now go left again on a road which takes you over a railway bridge and down into a wood.

When you come out of the wood, turn right and come to the first houses of Seugy.

The GR1 goes through part of the village. Take a path which runs through vegetable gardens and brings you to a road on which you turn right.

Warning The itinerary may be changed: pay careful attention to the waymarkers.

Go under the railway bridge (SNCF stop). Turn left onto a road which follows the railway track and then the golf course. After a bridge, turn first right and then left. Branch off to the left in a wide avenue. At a place called Saint-Côme, go down the metalled road. Now take the Rue du Cygne till you come to the old covered market of Luzarches.

When you reach the market, turn right into an avenue and continue over the bridge across the N16. Now, turn immediately left onto a road running parallel to the N16.

Turn right along the edge of the meadow till you come to a road. Pass in front of a former bleaching plant and then turn immediately left onto a road shared with a PR. This brings you into the forests of Coye and Orry, where you turn right.

To the left, there is a junction with the Circuit PR (petite randonnée) de Luzarches (yellow waymarkers) which follows the same route as the GR as far as the Carrefour de la

9Km
2:30

largely state-owned. Oaks predominate and, in spring, there is lily of the valley, wild hyacinth and wild strawberries.

Ménagerie. Cross one section, heading first north and then east.

At the Carrefour de la Ménagerie, the Circuit PR de Luzarches branches off to the left. Carry straight on. At the Carrefour du Parc-aux-Lièvres, there is a junction with the Circuit PR de Coye (yellow waymarkers). Carry straight on until you come to the Carrefour de Luzarches.

Turn left towards the Carrefour des Moines. Head right to the Carrefour du Chêne Sec. Turn left into the Route Nibert. At the entry to Coye-la-Forêt (Coye detour), there is a junction with the PR de Coye. Turn right onto the D118 and go under a railway bridge close to the Gare d'Orry-la-Ville-Coye.

GARE D'ORRY-LA-VILLE-COYE
☥ 🍷

Detour

2Km
0:30

Outside the station, turn left and go to the bridge.

After the bridge, turn left and follow the railway line. Take the first turning to the right towards the Carrefour des Grandes Ventes. Branch off to the left on the Route Forestière du Champoleux until you come to the Carrefour Saint-Ladre. Turn off to the right on a track that will bring you out above the pools of Comelle. Go down to the first pool, passing on your left the Château de la Reine Blanche.

Château de la Reine Blanche

This pseudo-Gothic edifice was constructed in 1828 by the Duc de Bourbon as a hunting lodge. It was built on the site of a château said to have been occupied around 1350 by Queen Blanche of Navarre, the wife of Philippe IV of Valois.
Starting point of the GR12, an itinerary which forms part of the European walk E3.

4Km
1:00

Go past the Maison Forestière de la Reine Blanche. Follow the left bank of the first, second and third pools.

Turn left onto the causeway between the third and fourth pools. Bear right along the fourth. Follow the right bank of the River Thève till you come to the road. Turn right here and come out of the woods to reach the hamlet of Montgrésin.

MONTGRÉSIN
🏠 ✗ 🍷

Cross the D924A and take the track opposite, along the edge of the meadow. Take the first turning on the left to come to the beginning of the Forêt de Chantilly.

The forest has changed hands many times, passing

Go north-east through the forest. Turn right and you will now come to the Maison Forestière de

Open country in the Île-de-France

3Km
0:45

from the Bouteiller family in the 14th century to the Chancelier d'Orgemont and then, in the 17th century, to the Montmorency and the Condé families. It was afterwards inherited by the godson of the Duc de Bourbon, the last Prince de Condé. Finally, Henri d'Orléans, Duc d'Aumale, the fourth son of Louis-Phillipe, donated it to the Institut de France.

PONTARMÉ
✕ ☖ ⚓ ▭

2Km
0:40

Junction on the left with the PR de Pontarmé (yellow waymarkers).

THIERS-SUR-THÈVE
✕ ⚓

la Vignette. Opposite the front door to the house, take the wide track between pines leading to the Carrefour des Tilleuls. Now take the Route du Château which is slightly to the right. At the corner of the château, turn left onto a road which brings you to the N17 at the edge of Pontarmé.

Go left along the N17 for about 100 metres. Turn off to the right and follow the road along a wall.

At the end of the wall, turn left before the bridge and follow a path to the Red Cross near the water tower on the way out of the village of Thiers-sur-Thève.

Turn left onto the gravel track leading into the Forêt d'Ermenonville.

The forest was created at the time of the French Revolution by uniting the woods belonging to the neighbouring abbeys of La Victoire, Chaalis and Saint-Sulpice.

Turn right onto the Route Vieille and then bear diagonally left to reach the top of the Butte-aux-Gens d'Armes (102m).

**7.5Km
2:20**

This sandy knoll overlooks the east of the Forêt d'Ermenonville and, in Capetian times, it was from here that the Gens d'Armes carried out their inspections of the four 'pays': France to the south-east, Parisis to the south-west, Valois to the north-east, and Beauvaisis to the north-west.

Go down to the right and turn left onto the Route Vieille once again. Turn off to the right after a few metres onto a gravel track running next to the A1, which you cross by a bridge. When you come to the Maison Forestière de la Pislote, turn right on the track next to the house. As the GR now changes direction several times, particular attention must be paid to the waymarkers.

At the Carrefour du Sycomore, turn right onto the Route Sainte-Marguerite.Then go right on the Route du Bosquet-Rond until you come to the Pavé d'Avesnes (D126).

Le Pavé d'Avesnes

Cross the D126 to the Poteau du Petit-Carrefour. Turn right here onto the Route Longue.

**3Km
0:45**

At the Carrefour du Hêtre, go south-west on the Chemin des Ermites, passing in front of the fences of the Château de Saint-Sulpice-la-Ramée. Cross the D922 and so come to the Route du Bois-d'Hyver.

Route du Bois-d'Hyver
Junction with the Ermenonville detour.
Detour *1 hr*
from Ermenonville to the GR
🏠 ⛺ ✕ 🍷 🚉 🚌

**1Km
0:15**

Detour see left. The starting point of the detour is on the D922 on the way out of Ermenonville. Follow the road to the junction with the D84 and then take the Route Forestière de Moret. At the Carrefour du Puits de Loisy, turn right onto the Route de Saint-Sulpice and then left onto the Chemin du Lièvre. Turn off onto the Vieux Chemin du Fouillis. Branch left onto the Route Longue and then go right on the Route du Bois-d'Hyver.

Turn right onto the Route du Bois-d'Hyver which brings you to Loisy.

Ermenonville

Ermenonville still lies under the spell of Jean-Jacques Rousseau's visit in 1778. You can visit the Château d'Ermenonville, the small park and the large Parc J.J. Rousseau. The gardens were laid out by the Marquis de Girardin who lived here in the second half of the 18th century. Putting into practice the ideas of Rousseau's 'Nouvelle Héloise', he proceeded to 'beautify nature' by transforming marshland into a romantic park of rocks, ruins and artificial streams.

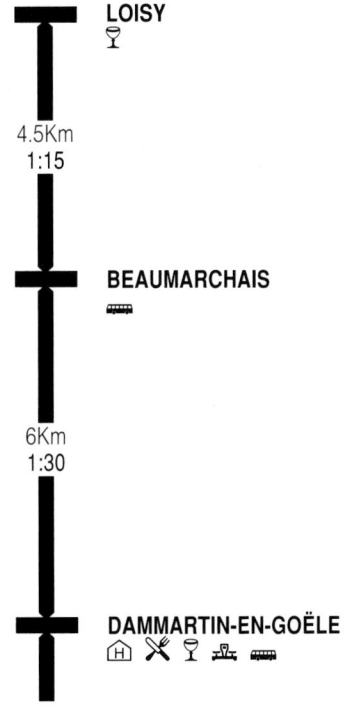

LOISY

Turn left onto a gravel track which brings you onto the local road from Loisy at Ver-sur-Launette. Go left for about 400 metres. Branch to the right.

4.5Km
1:15

Warning The itinerary may well be altered because of construction work for the high speed train system (TGV Nord). Pay particular attention to the waymarkings.

BEAUMARCHAIS

Go right on the D26E. On the way out of the hamlet, turn right on the Route de Plailly. Then turn left onto a track between the fields and then left again onto a wider tree-lined track leading to the Ferme de Saint-Ladre. Turn left here onto the D26E. When you come to a bend, take the track opposite up towards the hill. A winding path brings you to another track on which you turn left. Follow the ridge past the foot of a radar mast and then go down past La Corbie to reach the first houses of Dammartin-en-Goële.

6Km
1:30

DAMMARTIN-EN-GOËLE

Go directly across the D401 into the Rue des Oulches and then left on the Ruelle des Filoirs. Take the D13 to the right for about 200 metres.

Dammartin-en-Goële

The city of Dammartin-en-Goële has a long history. The fortified town was wrested from the English by Joan of Arc while on her way to lay siege to Paris. She was accompanied by the lord of the town, the faithful Antoine de Chabannes, whose body now lies in the collegiate church of Notre Dame. Traditions are maintained here so that you find, for example, companies of archers. The town was also the setting for one of the episodes in Gérard de Nerval's 'Sylvie'.

Visit the collegiate church, the Hôtel de Dieu hospital, the promenade and the ruins of the castle from where there are panoramic views over the Plaine de France.

Turn off on the first lane to the left and then almost immediately go right on a gravel track. The gravel changes to grass and the track crosses a gully before reaching the D404. Turn left here and continue along the road after passing under a bridge. Opposite a garage, turn left on a track which takes you to the D41B at the start of Saint-Mard.

SAINT-MARD
✕ ⚓ 🚉

1Km
0:15

Turn right into Rue Carnot and then straight along the Avenue de la Gare. At no. 73, turn left into an alley leading to the Place de la Gare de Dammartin-Juilly-Saint-Mard.

Gare de Dammartin-Juilly-Saint-Mard

4.5Km
1:15

Follow the railway line and cross by a bridge. Go along a wide track which bears off to the left. Then turn right into a grassy lane and under the electricity cables. Carry on straight ahead into the trees of the Bois de l'Homme-Mort and the Bois de l'Oratoire. Further on, follow the edge of the forest on your left. At a junction with a sunken lane, turn left. Then turn off on a lane to the right. This continues as the Rue des Blossiers and brings you into Montgé-en-Goële.

MONTGÉ-EN-GOËLE
⚓ 🚉 🚌

After the church, turn left into the Rue Neuve and then again into the Rue du Sépulcre. At the top of the hill, turn right and go between the cemetery and the reservoir to the foot of the TV mast. Go straight ahead on the tarmac road until you come to a bend. Leave the road and continue straight ahead through woods. Turn left onto a footpath and then right onto a forest road.

7.5Km
2:00

Turn right and cross the D9 onto the track opposite, continuing for about 2 kilometres. At a junction where the track widens out into a road, turn right and follow the track through the Bois de Saint-Soupplets. Then follow a wide dirt road across the plain, with the Étang de la Grue on your right. The surface changes to grass and then tarmac as the road rises. Towards the top, you will be able to see the Château de Monthyon over the walls of the estate.

MONTHYON
✕ ⚓ 🚉

At the church, go down the Rue Gambetta and across the Rue La Fayette (D97) into a dirt

5Km
1:15

The church has a solid early Gothic tower. In front of the door, there is a statue of M. de Monthyon, the 18th-century philosopher and economist, who used his immense fortune to endow the 'Prix Monthyon'.

PENCHARD
✗ ♈ ▦

2Km
0:30

CRÉGY-LES-MEAUX
✗ ▦

Junction with the GR1B (See Walk 3, page 131)

2.5Km
0:40

MEAUX
⌂ ✗ ♈ ▦ ▦ ▦ ▤

The town is rich in history and archaeology but is largely remembered for the fact that Bossuet, the Eagle of Meaux, was bishop here for 28 years and that it was also from here that Louis XVI and his family were returned after their abortive flight. Visit the cathedral of Saint-Etienne (12th and 15th centuries), the Old Chapterhouse (13th century), the Musée Bossuet, the ramparts, the garden of the bishop's palace.

5Km
1:15

road which skirts the buildings of the Ferme-Usine de l'Hôpital on your right. The road takes you into the Bois de Penchard. Turn right, then left, then right again. When you reach the D140, turn immediately left and follow a track running behind a housing estate. After about 400 metres, the track turns right and comes out on the D140 where it enters Penchard.

Take the N330 opposite for a few metres. Turn right into the Rue Lucien-Duquesne. Turn left into the Rue de l'Arpent-Noir. Go past the stadium and then, immediately afterwards, turn right onto a track. Cut across the D5 and then the D38 on the outskirts of Crégy. You now come to old Crégy.

Turn right and go down the Rue de la Roche. Cross the Canal de l'Ourcq and turn right. The road narrows and runs below the canal beside the Bois du Marais Saint-Faron. Turn right here to join the towpath which takes you under the N330. After a footbridge, turn left onto a tarmac footpath running down to the Rue de Senlis. Turn left at the traffic lights and then right under the railway bridge to reach the Gare de Meaux.

Outside the station, cross the square and car park and then go down the steps to the bank of the Marne. Carry on under the new bridge and then come up onto the Quai Victor-Hugo. Take the footbridge on your right to cross the Marne. Turn left on the covered quay. Cross the Rue du Commandant-Bergé and continue directly along the Quai Sadi-Carnot. 50 metres further on, turn left onto the promenade and continue along the edge of the gardens overlooking the Marne. Pass by the Pont-Neuf on your left and carry on until you come to the Quai Debèffles. Turn right along the canal as far as the N36. Cross the canal here and then turn left onto the Quai Maréchal-Mortier to come back to the Marne. Follow the track along the bank until you come to the Canal de Chalifert. Follow the track up to the N36, ignoring another track going off towards the locks. Cross the canal and turn left into a minor road leading to the Usine des Eaux.

Warning If the Marne is in flood, stay on this road until you return to the GR1 on the D17.

Where the road bends, take the grassy footpath down to the edge of the Marne. Now follow the tow path for 2.5 kilometres. Turn right off the river bank onto a track leading to the D17, where you again go right. At a junction, on the corner of the Cimetière de Nanteuil, turn left into the Rue de la Lampe. Continue to the Place de l'Eglise which you cross on the right. You now come to the junction with the D228 in the centre of Nanteuil-les-Meaux.

NANTEUIL-LES-MEAUX
✗ ♨ ☎

Junction with the GR14A which shares the route for about 200 metres.

Junction with the PR1 : circuit de Nanteuil-les-Meaux.

7.5Km
2:00

Turn left on the Rue Gambetta. Leave this road and continue directly ahead on the Chemin des Buttes. Now, bear right. Turn left and cross the Aqueduc de la Dhuys.

Take a minor road which you leave at the first bend, continuing straight ahead till you come to the D85. Turn left on this road and then right onto the D33 which takes you south over the A4 autoroute. Now, turn left onto the D87. Turn right onto a track which comes out on the D33. Turn left for about 30 metres. Now turn right and then left further on. When you come out of the wood, go straight ahead. At the end of the track, turn left and go up a slight slope into Bouleurs.

BOULEURS
♈ ♨

Turn right into the Rue de l'Eglise. Go through the hamlet of La Rue-de-l'Egout along the Rue de la République.Turn left into the Chemin de Rebais. At Férolles, take the D85 for about 300 metres.

4Km
1:00

Junction with the PR32: Circuit de Villiers-sur-Morin.

Shortly afterwards, turn right onto a track and continue until you come to a junction.

Junction with the PR30: Circuit de Crécy-la-Chapelle.

Turn right and then, after 400 metres, left onto a track going downhill. Cross a minor road and then the N34 before reaching the outskirts of Crécy-la-Chapelle.

CRÉCY-LA-CHAPELLE
⌂ ⚠ ✗ ♈ ♨ ☎ ☎
ℹ

Carry straight on along the Sente des Baulnes. Turn left onto the leafy promenade along the Fossé de la Ville.

Crécy-la-Chapelle
Several branches of the River Grand-Morin run through the town. Parts of the town's medieval wall are still to be seen. Of the 99 towers which it once boasted, only a few remain, one of these having been used as a studio by the painter Corot. The church of Saint-Georges, rebuilt at the end of the 18th century, still remains, flanked by a large Gothic tower, which houses the relics of several saints. 2 kilometres away, off the GR, you can see the Eglise de la Chapelle-sur-Crécy, a 13th-century church modified in the 15th century.

Detour *5 mins from the station. Outside the station, turn left on a street lined with lime- trees which runs into the Rue du Bon-Accueil.*

2Km
0:30

Junction at the cemetery with the PR29 and on the right with the GR de Pays des Morins.

Turn right and then left into the Rue Jean-de-Compans which continues as the Rue du Barrois and Rue Dam-Gilles (no. 28 is a 12th-century watch house). Now cross the Grand-Morin.

Go left on the D20 for 200 metres and then turn off diagonally right onto a track up to the plateau. (There may be no waymarkings for 500 metres.) You now come out onto a broad gravel track and turn right. At the first junction, turn left and descend the steep slope to the D20. Go left along the road for 100 metres and then turn right to cross the bridge over the Grand-Morin. You now come into Serbonne.

Serbonne

Warning If the river is in flood, stay on the road while passing through the hamlet.

After entering the hamlet, turn right into a public courtyard. Go down to the river bank and follow it to the left for 300 metres. Beyond a meadow, take the track on the left up to a farmyard (public right of way) and back to the road. Turn right and carry on up to the plateau. Go down to the right on the Route de Monthérand à Tigeaux. Turn off to the left on a dirt road. After crossing a grassy ridge, the path returns to the Grand-Morin and follows it a short way from the bank. You now come to a road opposite the Moulin de Coude.

6Km
1:30

Warning In rainy weather or when the river is particularly high, the GR1 may be impracticable on this stretch. If this is the case, cross over the Grand-Morin to the Place de l'Orme in the centre of Dammartin-sur-Tigeaux. Now turn left to join the waymarked detour described on p69.

The GR1 carries straight ahead, coming to a wide gravel track.

Junction with the PR30.

Turn right onto the gravel track. The GR de Pays des Morins now branches off towards Coulommiers. Turn right onto a track leading to the Grand-Morin, where you use the Prémol footbridge to cross over to the mill of the same name. On the right, you will find the detour to Dammartin-sur-Tigeaux.

Detour *15 mins*
from
DAMMARTIN-SUR-TIGEAUX
♟ ⚒

Detour see left. The point of departure is in the centre of the village in the Place de l'Orme. At the corner of the Rue du Pont-de-Coude (no. 2), follow the track between the gardens and the wall of a property. Continue uphill along the wall until you come to the altitude marker IGN 103. Here, the detour goes left down towards the Moulin de Prémol and the waymarkers of the GR1.

2Km
0:30

The GR1 now carries straight on to the Ferme de Prémol. Leaving the farm buildings on the left, turn right onto a gravel track going up to the plateau. Cross the railway bridge.

Junction with the PR28:
Circuit de Génévray.

Turn right and follow a track through orchards and copses for 800 metres. Turn off to the right on another track leading down to the D20.

D20

Cross over the D20 and the D20E, continuing straight ahead until you come to the railway. Before the bridge, turn left onto a track leading back towards the D20E. After a few metres, take the first track to the right and go under the railway line to reach the GR1.

2Km
0:30

Junction of GR14 and GR1
Detour *30 mins*
from the Gare de Montcerf.

Detour see left. Turn right towards the level crossing and then go immediately left. The GR14 follows a track below the railway line. It goes through a wood before coming to a minor road and passing under the railway viaduct.

The GR1 and GR14 run together for 2 kilometres.

2Km
0:30

Branch right and continue for about 300 metres. Where the road bends, leave to the right on the Route de l'Obélisque, a gravel track leading into the Forêt de Crécy.

Forêt de Crécy

The forest, which covers an area of 3,500 hectares, is gradually being acquired by the state as a public amenity. The GR1 winds along the edge of privately owned sections which are fenced off.

The forest flora is that of a rich damp soil formed from clay and silts. Oak coppices with standards predominate and there has been some planting of conifers.

Junction at first turning to the right with the PR29: Circuit des Trois-Châteaux.

Continue straight ahead and upwards on the Route de l'Obélisque to the separation of the GR14 and the GR1.

Separation of the GR14 and the GR1.

The GR1 goes through undergrowth on the left. After about 400 metres, turn first right and then left. Now turn immediately right onto the Route Philippe, which takes you south, crossing the D231. Turn left onto a footpath and then right onto a riding path which brings you out onto the Route de Penthièvre. Turn left on this road and, after 150 metres, turn off right on a footpath. Turn left on the Route Philippe and head south.

5.5Km
1:20

Junction on the right with the PR31: Circuit de la Forêt de Crécy.

Turn left on the Route Tournante to leave the Forêt de Crécy. After the road bends right, take the first lane on the left. Cross the D216 and the railway line. Turn right and continue till you come to the disused Gare de la Houssaye-en-Brie. Cross the D143E.

D143E
Detour *5 mins*
LA HOUSSAYE-EN-BRIE
✗ 🚆

3Km
0:45

Continue straight on, keeping the railway line on your right. As the itinerary may be modified, pay careful attention to the new waymarkers. Go over the second level crossing and cross back at the third. Now turn right onto the D143E and continue until you come to the cemetery of Marles-en-Brie.

MARLES-EN-BRIE
✗ 🚆 🚌

The GR turns right and follows a track along the cemetery wall. It then turns right before curving away off to the left. When you reach the junction with the D143E, turn right onto this road for about 20 metres.

Detour *15 mins*
Gare de Marles-en-Brie.
Continue along the D143E.
When you get to the N36,

The GR goes left along the Rue de la Croix-Saint-Pierre. Take the second turning on the right. The road continues as a track and crosses the former N36. Take the first track to

4.5Km
1:10

turn right and continue until you come to the Gare de Marles-en-Brie.

FONTENAY-TRÉSIGNY

⌂ ✕ 🚉 🚌

The church dates from the 15th and 16th centuries. The château is 17th century but two of the towers are older.

7Km
1:40

Take the first gravel track on the left to get to the ruins of the château. It was rebuilt by Charles V and Charles VI was kept here during his bouts of insanity.

CHAUMES-EN-BRIE

⌂ Δ ✕ 🚉 🚌

Home of Couperin, the great musician of the 17th century.

Junction with the GR de Pays de la Vallée de l'Yerres, coming from Combs-la-Ville.

4Km
1:00

VERNEUIL-L'ETANG

⌂ ✕ 🚉 🚍 🚌

the left, which runs parallel to the embankment of the disused Marles-Verneuil l'Etang line. Go through a small wood and then come to the junction with the N36. Turn right and continue on, crossing the N4 to come into Fontenay-Trésigny.

Warning As the itinerary may well be changed, pay close attention to the waymarkers.

Turn right in front of the church and go along the Rue Jehan-de-Brie. Turn left onto the D144A, which follows the wall of the château grounds.

Turn left onto a track leading to the Moulin du Pont. Now turn right on a footpath through bushes to the hamlet of Visy. Turn right. Cross over the channel of the Ru de Bréon and come back to the D144A. Turn left onto this road, which will bring you past the Château du Vivier.

Turn left onto a track, hedged on either side, which goes down between the grounds of Le Vivier and Ecoublay (convalescent home). Cross the Ruisseau de Bréon. Turn right along the stream and then proceed through woods and pasture to Chaumes-en-Brie.

Go round the cemetery. Now take the Rue Arthur Chaussy and cross the former N36.

Follow the Boulevard des Barres and then, after the Place Massa, go down the Boulevard Paulat for 100 metres. Turn right into the Sentier de la Brèche des Vignes. Take a right turn onto the promenade and then cross the viaduct over the Yerres. Cut across the D32 and follow the track directly opposite along the edge of the wood. Ignore the GR de Pays de la Vallée de l'Yerres which is on your left and instead bear right. At the first junction, turn left. When you are past the first houses, turn right into the Rue de la Gare at Verneuil-l'Etang.

Cross the road bridge and go left along the D47 for about 100 metres. Turn right into a

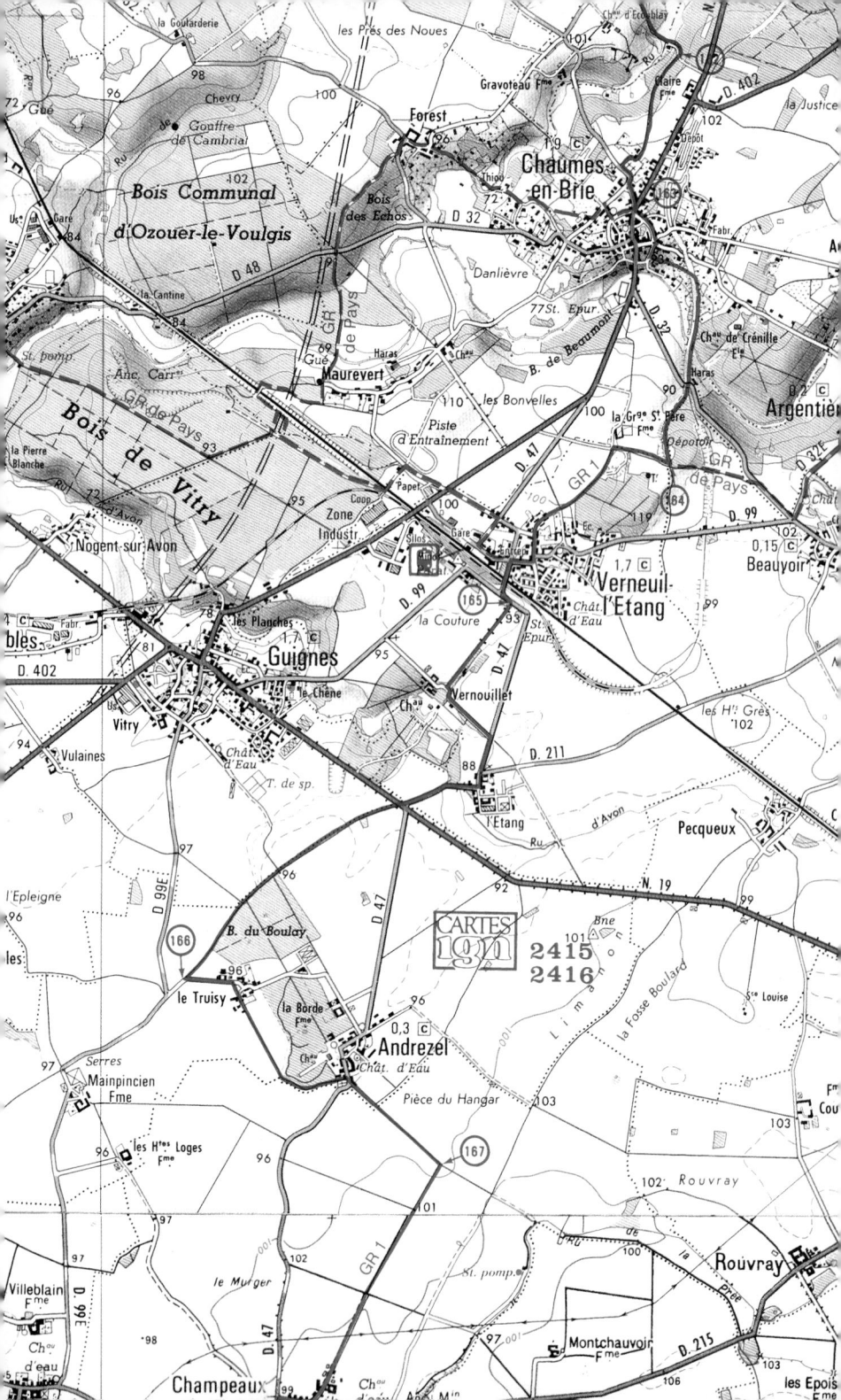

2.5Km
0:40

N19
Detour *30 mins*
GUIGNES

4Km
1:00

ANDREZEL

3Km
0:50

CHAMPEAUX

*Champeaux, founded by
Saint Fare in the 6th century,
was the home of Guillaume
de Champeaux, who was
first the master and then the
adversary of Abelard. A
fortified town grew up around
the collegiate church;
parts of the walls still remain.
The 12-13th century church
is built in a solid sober style.
See the stained glass
windows and the choir stalls
with their grotesque carvings.
Entry charge.*

7Km
1:45

BLANDY-LES-TOURS

*The village has one of the
few medieval castles to be
found in the Île-de-France;
hexagonal wall and imposing
14th-and-15th century towers
still remain. Views over the
surrounding countryside from
the top of the keep.*

broad tree-lined avenue, leading to the
Château de Vernouillet. Walkers are allowed to
use this private road by kind permission of the
owners. At the château gates, turn left on the
D47 and continue till you come to the N19.

Cross the N19 and follow the dirt road along
the edge of the Bois du Boulay. Turn left and
take the road to the hamlet of Truisy. As you
are coming in, take a dirt road without
waymarkers to the south-west corner of the
wooded grounds of the château. Carry on
along the edge until you come to Andrezel.

Beyond the cemetery, cross the D47 and follow
first the Rue des Marnières and then a track
for 900 metres. Turn right and, when you come
to a small junction with a cross, turn right
again onto the Rue de Varvanne. Once you
reach the D47, turn left and go through
Champeaux.

Cut across the D215 and turn right into the
Rue du Cloître. Now turn left into the Rue Sainte
Fare before turning right onto a farm track.

Turn left and then, 50 metres before you reach
a wood, go down to the right till you come to
the old Moulin de Flagy. Cross the d'Ancoeur
stream. After climbing up the other side, go left
and then right on a minor road for about 150
metres. You now come to a junction and go
straight across for a few metres. Turn right onto
a track heading south-east, and pass by a
small isolated chapel. Shortly afterwards, turn
right onto a broad track. Just before you reach
an electricity transformer, bear left. Further on,
take another track to the right. Next, go right
on the D47, to Blandy-les-Tours.

Turn left into the Rue Raoul-Kourinsky and then
left again into the Rue Vauchèvre. At no. 26,
go right on a track which crosses the TGV
railway line.

Turn right and carry on through meadows and
coppices. After passing the Tour d'Aiguillon,
the GR goes into the forest. Cross the channel
of the Ru de Bouisy below the Moulin de la
Roue. Turn right onto a paved road. After two

Blandy-Les-Tours

7.5Km
2:00

Vaux-le-Vicomte

The château was the precursor of Versailles and the greatest artists of the 17th century were engaged on the work of construction and decoration. Le Vau, Le

bends, turn right onto a footpath. Cross the D126 and then another tarmac road. A right turn at the Moulin de Pouilly brings you into Le Grand-Moisenay (church with 13th-century stone tower). Go left along the D215 to the entrance of the Château de Vaux-le-Vicomte.

Continue along the D215. After the château, take the first turning on the left. Turn right off this track onto another, which will bring you to the quarries. Now go down to the D82E, where you turn left and then cross the Ruisseau l'Almont to come into Maincy.

3Km
0:45

Brun and Le Nôtre all participated in creating this masterpiece for Fouquet, Louis XIV's superintendent of finances. The château is now the property of Comte Patrice de Vogüé.

MAINCY
✕ ⚓ ▭

Go through the village, turning right before the church onto a track leading to Trois-Moulins. After the last house, turn left and follow the cart track uphill. The track skirts woods and meadows until it comes to a minor road. Turn right here and continue till you cross the Ruisseau l'Almont. Now turn left and join the D117 which takes you under the N105. At a junction, turn left into the Rue des Petites-Fabriques and back across the Ruisseau l'Almont.

5Km
1:30

At the beginning of the Rue Flammarion, there is a break in the waymarking. You now come out into the Rue Saint-Liesne, almost within sight of the large and picturesque Place Saint-Jean at Melun.

MELUN
⌂ ⚑ ✕ ⚓ ▬ ▭ ℹ
hôtel de ville; Eglise Saint-Aspais which was damaged in the war; Eglise Notre-Dame; the public park, museum and the island on which the city was first established.

As there is no waymarking until the station, a city bus may be used for this stretch.

From the Gare de Melun, the route is shared with the GR2 for 6.5 kilometres.

6.5Km
1:45

Outside the station, turn right along the Avenue de la Libération till you come to the Seine. Turn right along the bank, passing under the railway bridge and going through the Port de la Rochette. Turn right and go uphill on a track which takes you over a level crossing. Now turn left on a footpath running parallel to the railway line and continue until you come to the beginning of the Forêt Domaniale de Fontainebleau.

Forêt Domaniale de Fontainebleau
The forest covers 16,982 hectares, without counting the additional 3,340 hectares of the Massif des Trois Pignons.

The GR2 now branches off left to Montereau.

Bear right and take the Route de la Ruelle. At the Carrefour de la Table-du-Roi, cross the N6. Now take the Route Peraut and cross the D115. From here, follow the Route de la Table-du-Roi.

■
3.5Km
1:00

At several points, the GR1 cuts across the TMF (Tour du Massif de Fontainebleau), which has white-and-green waymarkings.

Turn right onto a track leading to the Mare aux Evées but return almost immediately to the previous road on which you again go right. When you come to the Route des Monts-de-Fays, turn right and continue on, crossing the Rocher Canon, till you reach the Route de Chailly à Samois.

Route de Chailly à Samois
Detour *50 mins*
from the Gare de Bois-le-Roi.

1.5Km
0:25

Detour see left. At the Place du Marché, turn into the Rue de la Paix and then go left into the Rue Pasteur. Next, turn right onto the Avenue de la Forêt and right again onto the Chemin des Coureurs. This takes you past the D138 and the N6 to Rocher Canon. Here, turn right onto the Route de Chailly à Samois where the GR1 waymarkers recommence.

From here, the GR1 heads directly south along the Route des Monts-de-Fays till it comes to the Route Tournante du Cuvier-Châtillon.

Fôrêt Domaniale de Fontainebleau

Route Tournante du Cuvier-Châtillon

Detour *3 hrs*
Fontainebleau-Avon.

🏠 ✗ ⚓ 🚌 🚃 ℹ

2Km
0:45

Detour see left (11 kilometres.) Turn left on the Route Tournante du Cuvier-Châtillon. Cross the Route des Monts-de-Truie. At the next junction, go right for 250 metres on a footpath leading to the Mare à Dagneau. On the plateau, turn left along a track which winds south. Descend to the right along the Route Christine.

Go left on the Route de Mory-de-Neuflieux and then on the Route du Luxembourg. At the Carrefour de Belle-Croix, turn right and follow the Route des Ligueurs south for 250 metres.

Turn left onto a path with blue waymarkers and continue until you come to the Route de la Vallée de la Solle where you again turn left. Turn right onto the Route de l'Union.

Take the Route d'Amélie to the Carrefour d'Amélie and the Maison Forestière de la Vallée de la-Solle. At the north-east corner of the camp site, turn right onto the Route de Buffon for 50 metres and then left along a path. Cross the N6 and continue straight ahead along the Route des Graviers, which rises towards the Rocher Cassepot.

The itinerary is shared with the yellow circuits of the PR des Amis de Samois.

Go right along a path, leading between the pools to the Carrefour Constantin. Now follow the line of the Vallée de la Solle and cross the D116. Take the footpath through the rocky western side of the Cassepot to the Tour Denecourt, from where there is a panoramic view over the forest. Follow the path down towards the Carrefour de la Tour Denecourt. Cross the Route de la Vallée de la Solle and follow a path which passes by the Désirée and Dorly fountains. Go down to the right on the Route Baudrillard and then turn right onto a road which follows the railway track. Cross the Avenue du Président-Roosevelt and go down to the Gare de Fontainebleau-Avon.

Go right for 300 metres on the Route Tournante du Cuvier-Châtillon, paying close attention to the waymarkers. The GR now comes to the Route de la Solitude.

Route de la Solitude
Detour *30 mins*
MAISON FORESTIÈRE DU BAS-BRÈAU
✕ 🚃

Head west on the Route du Cuvier-Châtillon and then turn left onto the road from Barbizon to Brolles.

The GR goes south along the Route de la Solitude to the Carrefour de l'Epine. Take the subway under the N6 and then follow the Allée des Artistes for 500 metres. Turn right to get to the Carrefour Félix-Herbet. Continue almost directly ahead on the Route de la Solitude which rises up onto the Platières d'Apremont. Once on the plateau, turn right and follow a footpath through the rocks to the Caverne des Brigands. Now go down to the left on the Route du Dormoir.

At the Carrefour des Gorges-d'Apremont, turn right onto a road with no name. Turn left onto the Route des Ventes-Alexandre. After about 450 metres, turn left onto a path over the rocks. Go down from here to a junction, which again has no name. Cross the Route de la Gorge-aux-Néfliers, leaving behind the rocks and plateaux of Apremont. Follow the Route du Puits-au-Géant and then turn off to the right on the Route du Fourneau-David.

8Km
2:30

Go along the Route des Trois-Frères and cross the D409. Turn left onto the Route du Monastère and then right onto the Route de la Roche-qui-Pleure. After crossing the Route de l'Ermitage, take the steps up to the Mare de Franchard.

Mare de Franchard

The route is shared with the GR11 for 200 metres. Follow a path leading to a fine prospect over the Gorges de Franchard. Cross the Route Raymond and come to the Antre des Druides. Shortly after this cave, go down to the right.

Turn left onto the Route Amédée and then left again onto the Route des Gorges de Franchard. Now turn right onto the Route des Ventes-Barbier.

8Km
2:20

Turn right onto the Route de Trévise and then continue along the Route Cavalière Cévise, which takes you to the Carrefour de la Touche-aux-Mulets. Go straight across onto the Chemin d'Arbonne à Ury and then turn right onto the

Route de la Rabouillère. Go right, first on the Route de la Gibelotte and then on the Route du Bois-Rond. Turn left onto the Route du Terrier, which brings you down into Gorge-aux-Archers.

Gorge-aux-Archers
Starting point of the path linking up with the GR13 and connecting the ends of the E3.

1.5Km
0:30

Go right on the Chemin d'Arbonne à Achères, which brings you to the D64 at Bois-Rond.

BOIS-ROND
✘

Cross the D64 and take the track towards the A6 autoroute. Go left along the edge of the A6 for a few metres and then under the road. Now take the Chemin de la Vallée des Potets for about 500 metres.

2Km
0:45

Turn left and come to the Vallée Ronde, where you turn right. When the path forks, bear left up into the rocks. You now come to a track in a valley and climb north for a few metres. The path comes out at a viewpoint towards the Trois-Pignons and connects with the Circuit Rouge des Trois-Pignons.

Circuit Rouge des Trois-Pignons

Descend towards the south over two rocky humps. Leave the red path and turn off to the right. Take the Chemin du Rocher-Fin and then go left along the Chemin de Melun. Cross the Chemin de la Vallée de la Mée. Pass by the TMF on your left and the red path on your right. Climb over the Grande Montagne and come down on to the Chemin des Béorlots.

5Km
1:30

Turn right along the Chemin de la Cathédrale and then right again on the Chemin du Rocher Cailleau. The GR comes back to the Chemin de la Vallée de la Mée on the left and enters Le Vaudoué.

LE VAUDOUÉ
✘ ⚓ 🍷

Go south out of the village and follow the D16A for 300 metres. Turn left on a track going up through a wood. Where the track forks, bear left and come to the plateau. On the left can be seen the ruins of a 12th-century chapel and a leprosarium, which is being restored.

At a crossroads, the GR turns right and heads west. Turn left onto the D16A and continue for

11Km
3:00

AUXY
À ✕ ♨

1Km
0:15

D63A
Junction with the GR32.

4Km
1:15

MALESHERBES
🏠 À ✕ ♨ 🚌 🛈

This old town once belonged to Jean de Montaigu who built the château. The estate passed to the D'Entraigues family and then to the D'Illiers before becoming the property of Chrétien de Lamoignon, whose son defended Louis XVI before the Convention. Château open to the public.
Eglise Saint-Martin dating from the 12th, 13th and 14th

6Km
1:30

1 kilometre. Now turn right and, at the first junction, climb left through undergrowth and come out on the road from Boissy-aux-Cailles to Tousson. Turn right here and, at the intersection (altitude marker 116), continue straight ahead on a track leading west southwest. To the right, you can see the church tower and water tower of Tousson.

When you come to a major junction of tracks, take the footpath through the briars. Turn right and then left before going off to the right on a track. A wide avenue on the left will now bring you to the D410. Cross the road and follow it down to the left. Just before the junction with the N152, take a short cut off to the right. When you come back to the N152, take care in crossing as visibility is restricted. Carry on up the hill and then turn left on the plateau along the edge of Auxy.

Turn right twice to pass through the village. Now descend to the left through the rocks. Take the road on your right for 150 metres and then turn off onto a broad sandy avenue. This brings you past a spectacular mass of boulders to the D63A.

Turn right on the D63A past the mountain-climbing school. The GR1 leaves the road and turns left along the Chemin du Marais, which takes you over the Essonne and to the D410. Take the passage under the road and continue to the church of Malesherbes.

Turn left into the château grounds.

At the top of the slope, bear right and cross the N152. Continue straight ahead and pass the Gare de Malesherbes before turning right on the D24. Turn left onto the D132 for just a few metres, immediately turning right and going downhill into the centre of Malesherbes past the tourist information bureau.

At a bend, turn left into the lane rising towards the Château de Rouville. Keep to the wall and continue directly ahead down to the hamlet of Rouville. Leave the hamlet by turning right in the centre and following the course of the

centuries. Inside, 15th-century sculptures.

Essonne for some way. After passing through the hamlet of Touvaux, you now come onto a road leading to Argeville.

Argeville

Go all the way through this prosperous hamlet to reach a crossroads.

Crossroads

Junction with the GR111 which shares the route towards Milly with the GR1 for 800 metres.
Detour *20 mins*
from the Gare de Boigneville.

3.5Km
1:00

Detour see left. Turn left and follow the railway line, which you cross by the first bridge on the left. Continue right, following the waymarkings of the GR111, on a minor road which passes the foot of the Butte de Châtillon. The GR1 is now to be found at the first junction.

Turn right and cross the Essonne at the Moulin Paillard. Turn left on a minor road for about 500 metres. The GR111 turns onto a track leading into undergrowth. In the wood, the GR1 turns left and rounds a sandpit. It now heads north and crosses a road. The track continues for 400 metres before rejoining the road and entering Buno-Bonnevaux.

Buno-Bonnevaux

At the east end of the church, note the Stone Age polishing stone.

Pass in front of the Place de l'Eglise and go over the crossroads.

Detour
from the Gare de Buno-Gironville.

Detour see left. Come out to the left of the level crossing and go either:
- straight on, towards Maisse, following the D1 for 1.8 kilometres and then going left on the Chemin de Grimery, or
- right, towards Malesherbes, following the road to Buno-Bonnevaux.

5.5Km
1:30

Turn right and go along the Rue de la Fontaine, the Rue des Sablons and the Rue de Milly. As you leave the village, turn left onto a track which brings you up to the road. Turn onto the Chemin de Grimery, the second track on your left.

Cross the D1 and continue along the Chemin de Grimery for about 2 kilometres, during

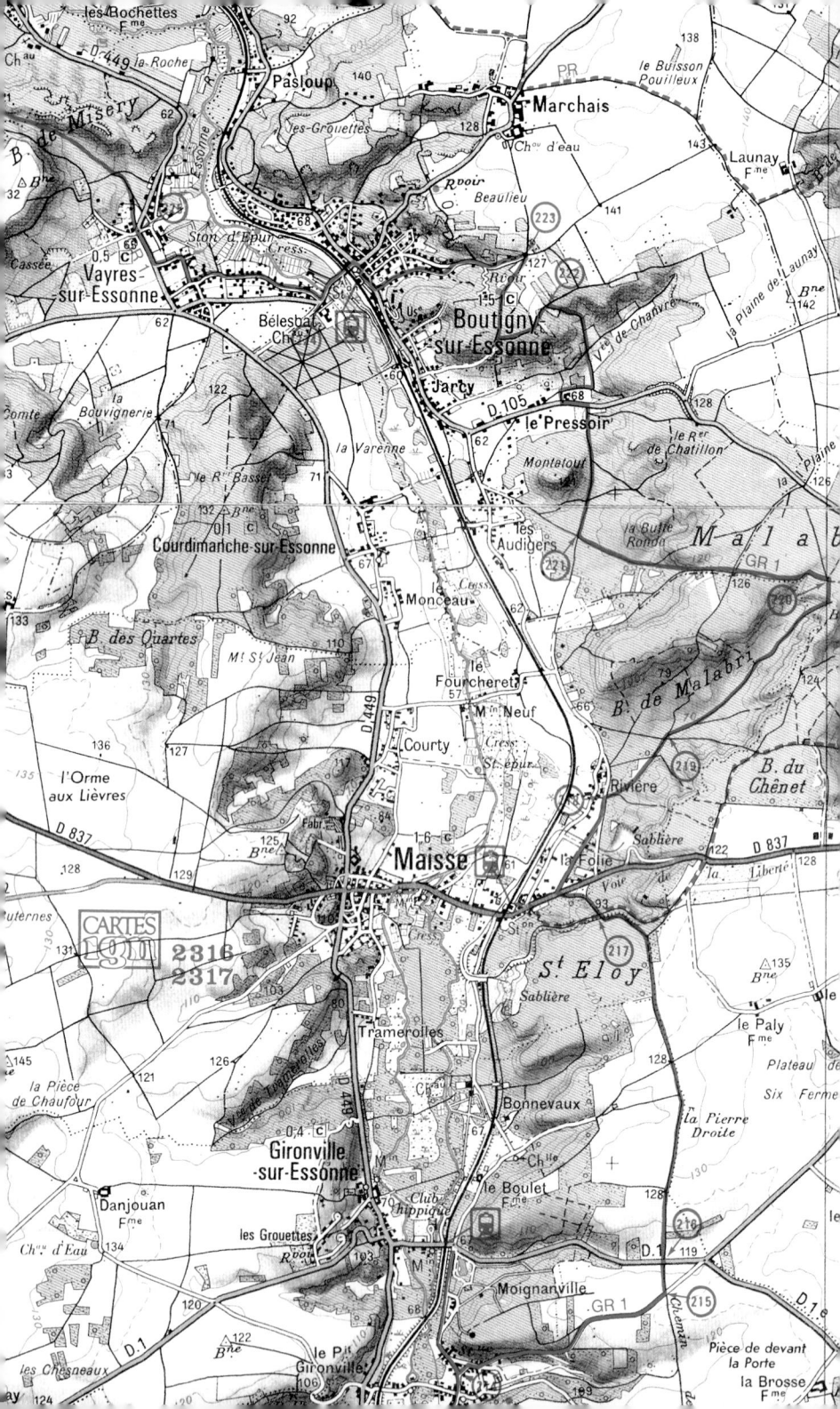

which there may be no waymarkings. Follow the edge of the wood, bearing left and then going downhill on the first track to the right. Cross a road at the junction with the PR de Milly-la-Forêt. Continue the descent and meet the D837 on the outskirts of Maisse.

MAISSE
🏠 🍴 🚉 💬

The centre of the village is 2 kilometres to the west.
Detour
from the station.
Go left on the D837 towards Milly. After about 500 metres, the GR1 and the D837 intersect.

From the top, at the Camp des Romains, there are panoramic views to one side over the Bois de Malabri and, beyond the River Essonne, the sandpits of Maisse. In the other direction, the church tower of Milly can be seen above the trees. To the left is Le Coquibus and, to the right, Mont Châteauveau, Mont Jean-des-Vignes and Mont Pivot, the three peaks of the Trois-Pignons.

11.5Km
3:00

Cross the D837 and follow the track past the houses of La Folie. In the Bois de Malabri, turn right off the track into an avenue. Turn right off the avenue and climb a slope through pines and birches.

Turn left onto a path that later widens out. At a crossroads, take the second track to the left. This leads onto another track which brings you to an altitude marker (126m). As you go down, turn right after a copse of false acacias. Cross the road which leads right to the Rocher de Châtillon and pass by the Butte de Montatout on your left.

Turn left for 150 metres onto the D105 which leads into the hamlet of Pressoir. Go round a farm and turn left onto the track through the Vallée de Chanvre. On the plateau, turn left. As you descend the path, turn right onto a broad track. At the edge of the woods, branch off to the left and go down towards Boutigny. The dirt road merges into the Rue de Cheval'Rue, which takes you to the D105. Turn left at the war memorial to reach the Gare de Boutigny-sur-Essonne.

BOUTIGNY-SUR-ESSONNE
🏠 🍴 🚉 💬

See the church with its solid tower and the Château de Belesbat.

2.5Km
0:35

Go past the station and the church before turning left onto the D153. Go over the level crossing and then the River Essonne to reach the Château de Belesbat, where the chancellor Michel de l'Hospital died in 1573. Turn right onto the Route de la Ruchère, which brings you into Vayres-sur-Essonne.

Vayres-sur-Essonne

5Km
1:30

LONGUEVILLE
(commune of D'Huison-Longueville)

5.5Km
1:30

BOISSY-LE-CUTTÉ

The GR follows the Route de la Ruchère as far as the war memorial. Turn right here into the Rue du Sourdet and then go right on the D449 for 250 metres.

Continue straight on and follow the Chemin du Four-à-Chaux into the Bois de Misery. Turn left into an avenue lined with pine trees and cross a broad sandy track. You now go through undergrowth for about 250 metres before turning right onto a track leading uphill. The itinerary cuts across a number of tracks, passing between two wooded knolls and bringing you to the fence of an army fuel depot. Continue along the track until you reach a nudist camp on your left.

The GR1 is joined by the GR111A coming from Puiselet-le-Marais at the corner of the camp wall. The two walks share the route for 2 kilometres. Turn right and follow the fence of the fuel depot. Cross the D145 and take the Rue d'Orveau into the heart of Longueville.

Turn left into the Rue de la Mairie and left again into the Rue du Fer-à-Cheval. Continue to the junction. Take the first turning on the left and leave the village towards the south-west on a track, which takes you first through fields and then woods.

At the top of the hill, the GR111A goes right in the direction of La Ferté-Alais. Carry straight on through fields and woods.

Before you come to the Boissy-Orveau road, turn right onto a path through holiday home properties. At the tip of a wood, take a track going north over fields. There are no waymarkers for 1 kilometre as there is nothing to attach them to. The waymarking resumes at the entry to a wood. Follow the edge of a quarry and then descend a slope to join the path leading to La Grande-Mare. This brings you out onto an esplanade, amid pines and jumbled sandstone. The path then leads down to the Rue des Vallées in Boissy-le-Cutté.

The GR1 and the GR11 share the same route for the 4 kilometres to La Roche-Fortière.

Junction with the GR11, which branches off left to Etréchy.

Cross the Longueville to Boissy road and continue straight ahead along the Rue du Maréchal Foch. Turn right onto a road leading to market gardens. Cross the gardens by a track, which brings you to the N191 at the entry to a camp site. Turn right and follow the N191 for 300 metres.

5Km
1:15

Turn left onto a forest path which continues as a track, running between market gardens.

Just before entering a pine wood, turn right along the edge and continue till you come to a country lane. Turn left and follow the lane for 75 metres before turning right onto a forest track. Cross over the road from Cerny to Orgemont and follow the path as it bends left. Within sight of the Château d'Orgemont, head off right, passing through a coppice and crossing a field (no waymarkers). You now come to another coppice. Turn left and go uphill to a place called La Roche-Fortière.

La Roche-Fortière

The GR11 now branches off right towards La Ferté-Alais. Take the left fork on the Chemin de Lardy, which leads to the D56. Cross the road and enter Le Petit-Boinveau.

2Km
0:30

Le Petit-Boinveau

Go past the houses of the hamlet. When the road forks, bear right and continue up to the plateau. Turn right onto a farm track, passing a half-buried water tank on the right. In front of the Ferme de Pocancy, turn right onto the road. At the beginning of a slope, turn off left onto a road through the Parc de Pocancy housing estate.

3Km
0:45

Turn right onto a track and cross a quarry to the left. Close to a little house, descend the steep slope on the right. At the bottom, turn right onto a path overlooking the first houses of Janville-sur-Juine.

JANVILLE-SUR-JUINE

Take the road to the left. Turn right onto the D17 and immediately turn left into the Rue de Goujon. This crosses the River Juine and brings you into Lardy.

. 1Km
0:15

LARDY

Turn left onto the D146 and, after 50 metres, turn off to the right on the road leading to the

station. Go through the subway and turn left onto a steeply rising gravel track.

Once on the plateau, turn left just before a restored farmhouse. Go through the woods and then turn off right for a few metres on a path at right angles. Now turn off on the first track to the left. This brings you out above a quarry which you follow for a good way before branching right and going through woods to the bottom of a valley.

**3.5Km
1:00**

Turn right and for 300 metres follow a stream running through a channel. Turn left onto a cart track and continue to an S-bend in the stream. Here, go uphill to the right. At a sewage treatment plant, turn left onto a track and head for the church at Torfou.

Torfou
11th-century church.

Just before the church, turn right and follow the wall of the grounds of the château. Leave the road and continue ahead for 50 metres. Take the first track to the left across country to where it ends in a wooded cutting. Turn left up the cutting and continue straight ahead for 1.2 kilometres before crossing the D99.

After a wood, turn right and come to the N20, which you cross by the bridge. Turn right up the N20 for 300 metres. With the D99 from Torfou in front of you, turn left onto a track towards some storage sheds. Level with the sheds, turn away from Mauchamps and go diagonally right, following the electricity pylons.

**6Km
1:45**

Detour *10 mins*
MAUCHAMPS
Little 15th-century country church with 18th-century panelling.

Turn right onto a track and go straight ahead. Bear left at a crossroads in the wood. From the top of a slope, with a fine view over the church of Saint-Sulpice-de-Favières, the GR descends past a school and comes out on the road from Mauchamps. You now go into Saint-Sulpice-de-Favières.

Saint-Sulpice-de-Favières

Turn right at the church and keep the grounds of the Château de Segrez on your left. Turn left onto a track which follows the other side of the grounds. Bear diagonally right on a track rising towards the Butte de Baville. After the gate marked 'Ker Jacques', the route of the GR1 follows local roads between private properties.

Saint-Sulpice-de-Favières

The village lies in a hollow between wooded hills and is dominated by a church of remarkable size for so small a place. The church is dedicated to Saint Sulpice, who became archbishop of Bourges in 647. It is here that he is reputed to have brought a drowned child back to life. Formerly a place of pilgrimage, the church still sees a ceremony of commemoration every 1st September.

The main structure is 13th-century but the Chapelle des Miracles dates from a century earlier. The two 13th-century stained glass windows are very fine, as are the misericords of the choir stalls.

The exceptional charm of the building was already recognised in the 18th century, when it was described by the Abbé Chastelain as 'the most beautiful village church in the whole kingdom'.

Two points should be borne in mind:
- Do not leave the path or go into the woods.
- Walkers have right of way here and no-one, not even a property owner, can challenge their free access.

Branch off, first to the left and then immediately afterwards to the right. Pay close attention to the waymarkings in the Bois de Baville. When you come out of the wood, the track goes over two fields so there are no waymarkers.

5.5Km
1:30

Turn right and go into a wood.

In the reverse direction: when you leave the wood, follow the path left along a hedge until you come to a farm track. Carry on straight ahead and then take the first track to your right, which goes up towards the Bois de Baville (no waymarkers). After passing under a little bridge, you come to the outskirts of Saint-Yon and then to the chapel of the same name.

Chapelle de Saint-Yon, the burial place of Saint Yon, a disciple of Saint Denys, who brought Christianity to the region.

Pass through the ruined Porte Bordeaux. The track now continues downhill through sand before crossing a road. Carry straight on between the restaurant and the riding centre. Cut across the D82 and over the River Renarde to reach Breux.

Breux

Detour *15 min from the Gare Breuillet-Village.*

Detour see left. Coming from Paris, leave the station and head for the level crossing. Turn right. Cross the River Renarde and then turn first left and next right. At the bottom of the slope, you come to the road and GR1

5.5Km
1:15

MIRGAUDON
Junction with the GR111D and the GR11.

Detour *15 mins*
Gare de Saint-Chéron.

7Km
2:00

waymarkings in the heart of Breux. Go right towards Dourdan or straight ahead towards Lardy.

Turn left onto the road and then, when it begins to go right, turn off on a dirt road and pass below Breux cemetery. Where the road forks, bear left and continue till you come to the tarmac road from Jouy to Rimoron. Turn right onto this road for 200 metres. Turn left onto a farm track along a wall. With the Bois de Chantropin on your left, continue until you reach the crossroads on the way into Mirgaudon.

Going south, the GR1 and the GR11 share the same route for 1.3 kilometres.

Detour see left. Leave on the side opposite the station building and follow the GR11 waymarkers. Outside the subway, turn left along the road following the railway track. Turn right and cross the River Orge, going up into Mirgaudon by the Rue du Gué At the end, turn left into the Rue de Chantropin where you will find the GR1 markers.

Follow the path uphill between the Bois de Chantropin and the Bois de la Butte-à-Moret. This brings you out onto a road, which you follow for 500 metres. Turn off to the right on the first asphalt road. Take the D132 for 200 metres to the edge of the hamlet of La Petite-Beauce.

The GR11 branches left, away from the GR1, passing the farm and heading towards Souzy-la-Briche and Etréchy. The GR1 continues along the D132 before turning off to the left on a tarmac road towards Saint-Evroult.

Turn left onto a track, which heads back before turning right. Before coming out onto the plateau, turn right onto a track which takes you to the edge of a meadow. Now continue along the footpath following the side of the slope. The path brings you onto a gravel section of track, leading to the plateau and fields.

Turn right and follow the edge of some rows of trees. Now go through the wood for a few hundred metres. When you come back to farmland, bear off slightly to the right and continue towards Mesnil. Go right for a short way and then turn left into the Rue du Mesnil. Opposite a pool, turn right onto a cart track leading to a wood. Turn left along the edge of the wood and then follow a footpath through a disused sandpit. Turn right and go a few metres down the Chemin Sermaise-Blancheface. Turn left onto a path which leads up the slope along the edge of the fields. Now turn right and go down through the woods to Sermaise.

SERMAISE

Detour *10 mins*
from the Sermaise stop.
When you leave the stop, go
straight ahead on the track
leading to Bellanger. Turn left
to reach Sermaise and the
waymarkers of the GR.

Pass by the church on the right. When you leave the village, turn left onto a farm track, leading up to the plateau. Follow the edge of the wood and a fence. Turn right onto a road towards the Ferme Villeneuve. Branch right onto a track leading to the village of La Bruyère. Carry straight on for about 100 metres.

Before going down, turn left onto a farm track leading to the woods. Skirt the woods and then take a track leading to Marchais. At the entry to the village, turn right onto the D148. At the first bend in the road, turn off onto a path which takes you down to a crossroads.

8Km
2:15

Junction with the PR de
Roinville-Châteaupers.

The GR crosses the D148 and continues straight ahead on a track past meadows, woods and fields. When you come to a crossroads, go past the Oray factory. At the next crossroads, turn right onto the Route du Pont Guénée. Cross the stream flowing from the Etang de la Muette and then the River Orge. You now come close to the swimming pool at Dourdan. From here, the GR follows the Rue Gaston-Lesage, the Avenue de Paris, the Rue Gautreau and the Boulevard des Alliés, the Avenue Carnot and the Avenue du Docteur Jules-Bals, which brings you to the Gare de Dourdan.

DOURDAN

The former capital of the
Hurepoix, Dourdan stands on

Warning The GR waymarkers on the right hand side of the footbridge are those of the GR111 towards Saint-Chéron.

the banks of the Orge. In the middle of the town, there is a castle with 13th-century walls, towers and keep. During the Hundred Years' War, the castle served both as a military stronghold and as a prison for Joan of Arc's companion, La Hire. It played the same dual role during the Wars of Religion. Later, particularly under the Empire, it was used mainly as a prison. Today, it is a museum.

7Km
2:00

The church dates from the 12th and 13th centuries; the left doorway is in flamboyant Gothic style. The building suffered damage in the fighting which took place around the castle.

SAINT-ARNOULT-EN-YVELINES

Å ✕ ⚓ ▭ 🏛

12th-century church, in flamboyant Gothic style, modified during the Renaissance; old wash-houses; Museum of Art and Popular Traditions.

For the 100 metres or so from the Gare de Dourdan to the beginning of the Rue du Faubourg-de-Chartres, the same route is shared by the GR1 and the GR111 to Etampes. Outside the station, go straight ahead down the Rue A. Guénée. Turn right into the Faubourg-de-Chartres (D116), which takes you out of the town.

For the 3 kilometres or so from the bridge to the Carrefour de Marcoussis, the GR1 follows the same route as the PR de Dourdan-Sainte-Mesme, which has yellow waymarkers. Turn right and take the passage under the railway line. Head off diagonally left on the track past the Stade de Dourdan, first on tarmac and then gravel. This takes you into the state forest of Saint-Arnoult. The track climbs up to the plateau as far as a sand hill, where you turn left. Turn right onto a track up to the Carrefour des Buttes-Blanches. Go straight across onto a forest avenue leading to the Carrefour du Grillon. Continue straight ahead on the Route La Lieue to the Carrefour de Marcoussis.

The PR de Dourdan-Sainte-Mesme branches off at this point. The GR1 now turns right and follows a forest avenue leading to the Carrefour du Beau-Chêne. Continue straight on to the next junction, where you turn left onto another avenue bringing you to the Carrefour du Rendez-Vous. You now pass under the railway and autoroute and follow the D836 for about 300 metres. Turn right onto the Route de Beauluisant towards the water tower. Carry straight on along the Rue de l'Isle and the Rue du Coq. Just after no. 5, turn left into a narrow alley which leads up to the church of Saint-Arnoult-en-Yvelines.

Go round the church and straight ahead into the Rue du Billoir. After crossing the Rue des Remparts and passing the Rue Laguesse, turn right onto the Sente des Mulets.

The GR1 now shares the route for a few metres with the PR6.

Cross the former Paris-Chartres railway line. After the bridge, turn right onto the track that

Forêt de Rambouillet

This is part of the old Forêt des Yvelines, which once covered the whole south-west of the Paris region. What now remains is the Forêt des Quatre-Piliers, the Forêt de Rambouillet, the Bois de la Celle, the Bois des Bordes, the Bois des Fonds de Bullion, the Bois de Saint-Benot, the Bois de Rochefort, the Forêt de Saint-Arnoult and the Forêt de l'Ouÿe.

The massif, covering 20,000 hectares, is divided in two by the town of Rambouillet. The forest itself covers 13,000 hectares and is in three main sections: Yvelines to the east of the town, Rambouillet to the west and Saint-Léger between the latter and Montfort-l'Amaury.

The forest occupies a plateau with an altitude of 180m, more rugged terrain lying to the north. It consists largely of coppice-wood with standards, primarily oak together with birch and Norway pine. The undergrowth is often filled with ferns and heather.

The ground is moist with many streams, ponds and pools and game is abundant. Lily of the valley and mushrooms grow in some areas.

6Km
1:30

Moutiers

runs parallel to the line. Cross the D27E and continue straight ahead to a housing estate. Turn left onto a tarmac road, which continues as a gravel track. When you come to a sand pit, turn left onto a winding path through woodland. Come out onto a larger track and turn right. Follow the edge of a wood and then go into the undergrowth, keeping a fence on your right.

Warning The right of way applies only to the country road.
Do not enter the wood.

Cross the D27 and enter the Forêt de Rambouillet.

Go straight ahead on the Route Sainte-Anne, a path with few markers. Follow the fence marking the boundary of the Domaine de la Claye. This will bring you out of the forest on a tarmac road, the Chemin de la Haye-de-Rochefort. You now come into Moutiers.

This is the starting point of the PR5 (white-and -blue waymarkings) which leads through La Celle-les-Bordes to the Poteau des Enclaves.

After 100 metres, the PR comes to the Chapelle Sainte-Anne and then, immediately afterwards, by a wash-house, to the Fontaine

Sainte-Anne with its statue of the Virgin Mother.

Turn left onto the Route des Yvelines (D132), which you follow to the lodge at La Claye. Where the road turns left, branch off to the right, following a forest avenue. When you come to Sainte-Scariberge signpost, continue straight ahead first along a fence and then along the Mare aux Douins. Cross the D72 at the Carrefour Messire-Jean and so reach the Carrefour de Goursac.

8Km
2:00

Junction on the left with the PR4 de Clairefontaine.

The GR now comes to La Croix-du-Grand-Veneur and a crossroads with the same name. Take the first track to the right and cut successively across the Route du Haut-Levé and the Route du Chêne-Quinquet, before reaching the Route du Parc de la Verrerie. Turn left onto this road for 300 metres. At the Carrefour du Chevalier-Quiqui, turn right and continue to the Carrefour des Enclaves.

Carrefour des Enclaves
Junction with the PR5 coming from Moutiers (white-and-blue waymarkings).
Detour *30 mins*
Hauts-Besnières
⌂
Opposite, follow yellow waymarkers of the PR to the gîte d'étape at Hauts-Besnières.

The GR heads left on the Route des Enclaves, crossing a road and then the N306. At the Les Hogues signpost, go right for 250 metres along the former Route de Chasse. Turn left into the undergrowth and follow a sunken lane along a fence. Now turn left onto a metalled road, which will take you across the Route Saint-Georges and on to the Etang de la Tour. Cross the N306 once again and continue along the Route de Batonceau. Cross the D27.

At the Carrefour de Villeneuve, turn right off the Route de Batonceau and follow a track for 100 metres. Now turn left onto a muddy path running parallel to the River Drouette. At the north end of the Etang d'Or, cross the Drouette and go diagonally left on a footpath which follows the edge of the pool.

10.5Km
2:30

Junction with the PR4 de Clairefontaine.

The GR1 goes through the Bois Domanial des Eveuses. When you come out of the forest, turn right into the Rue du Château-d'Eau. At the first crossroads, go under the N10 bypass. Continue straight ahead along the Rue des Eveuses to the railway bridge next to the Gare de Rambouillet.

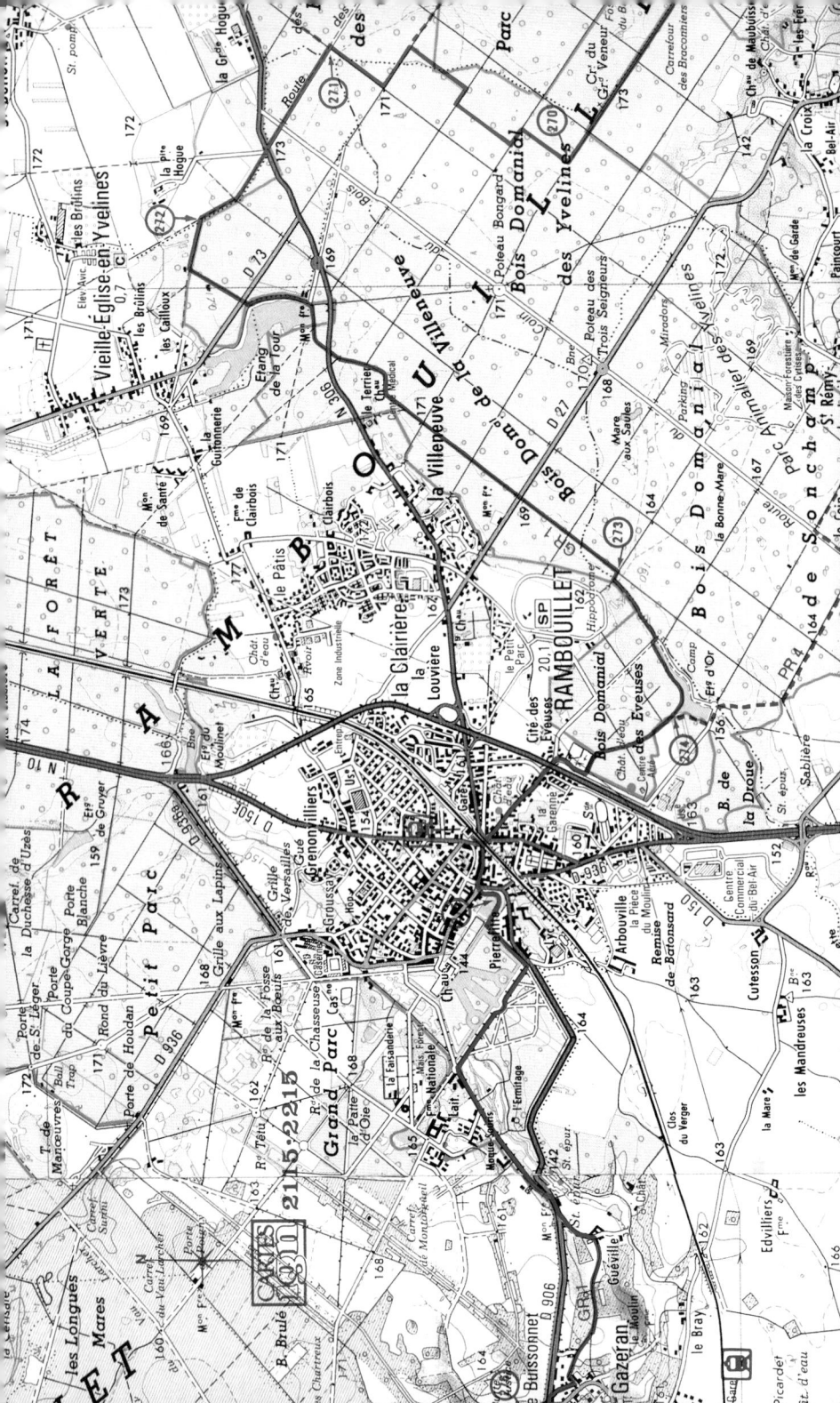

Rambouillet

The first reference to Rambouillet appears in 768. In 1612, the title of marquess was granted to the owner of the estate, Charles d'Angennes, husband of Catherine de Vivonne, the celebrated Marquise de Rambouillet. It was then made a royal dukedom for the Comte de Toulouse, a son legitimised by Louis XIV. In 1784, the château was acquired for Louis XVI.

Sights in town: hôtel de ville dating from the period of Louis XVI and housing the monumental map on which the king worked; the sous-préfecture, formerly a bailiwick; the Pavillon de Toulouse, a hospital in the 18th century.

The château is open to the public except when the president is in residence. Over six centuries, it has witnessed many historic events, including the death of Francis I in 1547. It was extensively modified during the last century. Visits can be made to the royal apartments of Louis XV with their 18th-century panelling and to Napoleon I's rooms and exotic bathroom.

In the grounds, you should see the small and large parks with their parterres, the French park, the avenues of Louisiana cypresses, the English garden, the grotto, the shell cottage, Marie-Antoinette's dairy and the Rambouillet museum. Here the sheep farm breeds world-famous merinos, descended from those purchased from Spain by Louis XVI in 1786.

RAMBOUILLET

5.5Km
1:30

Follow the Rue de Chasles to the château gates and enter the park. (If the château is closed, follow the D906.) Go through the park and leave by the Guéville gate. Cross the D906 and turn left onto a track leading towards Guéville. After a short way, turn right. Ignore a track to the left and come to the hamlet of Le Buissonnet.

LE BUISSONNET

Go left on the D906 for 50 metres. At the first crossroads, turn right.

Junction on the left with the PR2 de la Drouette (white-and-blue waymarkings).
Detour *30 mins*
Gare de Gazeran via the PR.

At a fork in the road, bear left and then, further on, right. Enter a section of the Forêt de Rambouillet called the Bois de Gazeran. Following the Vallée Drouin, keep the wire fence on your right. At the crossroads, turn right and continue along the fence.

Turn left onto the Route de la Pocqueterie. At the Carrefour du Bois-Dieu, go diagonally right on the Route Renée. At the Brèche-de-Poigny signpost, turn left onto the Route des Etangs d'Angennes. At the Carrefour des Rabières junction turn left at Circuit PR1 de la Forêt de Rambouillet (yellow waymarkings). The GR1 and the PR share the same route as far as the Carrefour du Four-Guérin.

5Km
1:15

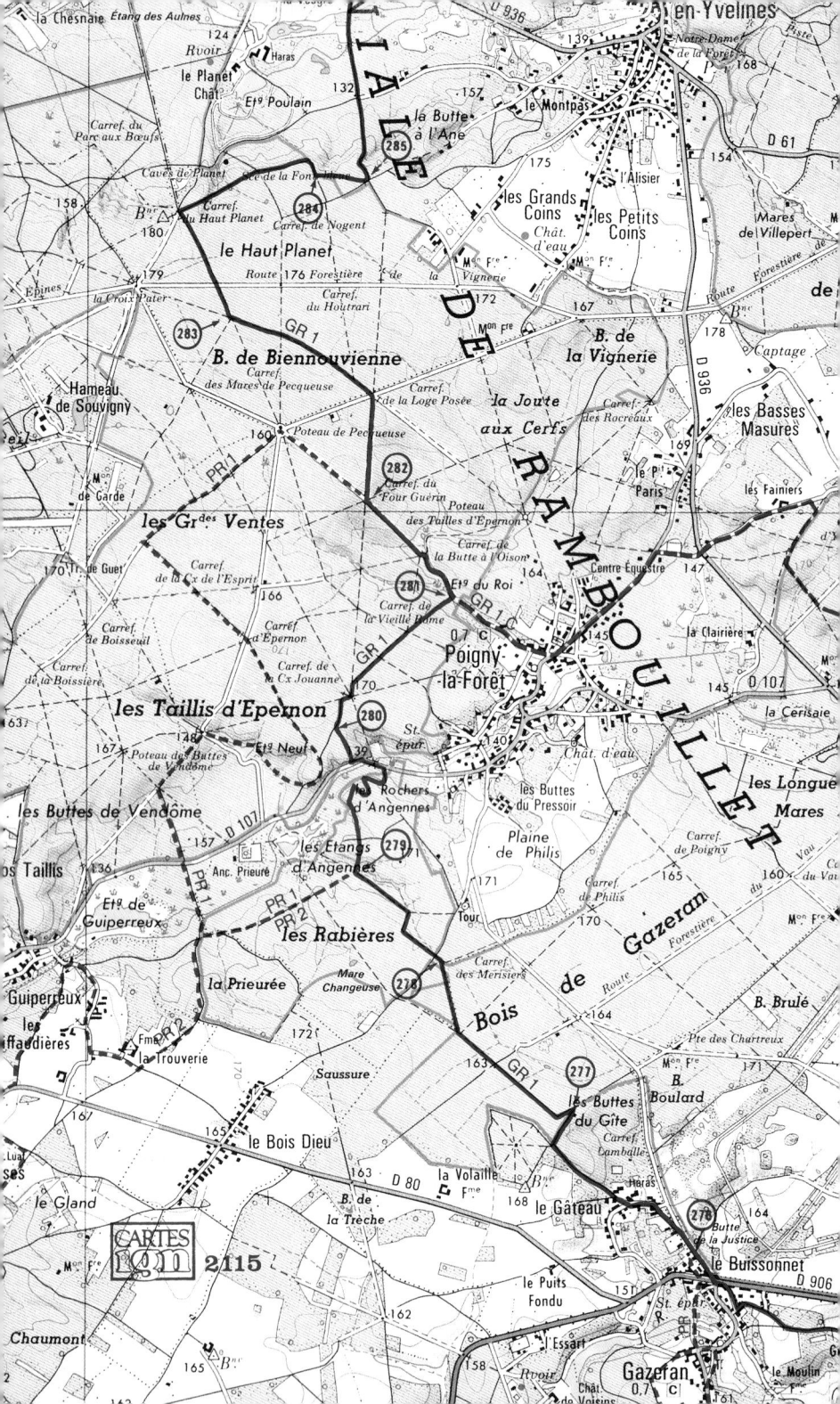

The Carrefour des Rabières is also the end of the PR2 from Saint-Hilarion (white-and-blue waymarkings).

Turn right onto the Route des Rabières which climbs up to the plateau formed by the Rochers d'Angennes. Then turn left onto a track leading down, and immediately turn off to the right on a footpath through the bracken, which brings you to an esplanade. Follow the paths along the north-west side of the plateau to a flat area overlooked by rocks to the right.

Take the footpath down through the bracken to a car park where you turn left onto the D107.

D107

Cross the River Guesle and turn right onto a track up through the rocks. Once on the plateau, turn right and follow the waymarked paths to the Route de la Mouche. Turn right and follow the road, passing close to the Carrefour de la Croix-Jouanne. Continue straight ahead on the Route de la Mouche to the Carrefour du Roi de Rome. From here go down to the Etang du Roi.

2Km
0:30

Etang du Roi

Junction on the right with the GR1C, leading to Perray-en-Yvelines.

Turn left onto the road along the pool and carry on till you come to the enormous forest junction of the Carrefour du Four-Guérin.

The PR2 continues straight on from here towards the Pecqueuse signpost.

Go diagonally right on the Route de la Gaudronnerie till you come to the La Loge-Posée signpost. Now turn left and take the Route de Rambouillet. At the Carrefour du Gros-Chêne, turn right and follow the GR across the Route de la Vignerie to the Carrefour du Haut-Planet.

The Forêt de Rambouillet is twinned with the Black Forest, as indicated by the reference to the 'Forêt Noire' on the signpost. This was added in 1968, when an oak from the Canton des Longues Mares was planted in the Black Forest, while a Black

10Km
3:30

Turn right onto the Route du Haut-Planet. At the Carrefour de l'Archet, cross the Route des Masures to reach the Butte de l'Ane. A few metres further on, turn right onto the Route de Biennouvienne.

Turn left onto a track with wire fences on either side. Turn left and left again. Disregard the notices saying 'Private Property' and take the

Forest pine presented in return by the Schwarzwaldverein was planted here on the Esplanade in a little coppice by the forest hut.

Château de Pincourt
Detour
10 mins
Saint-Léger-en-Yvelines
🏠 🍴 🚉 🚌

2Km
0:30

Turn left onto the Route de la Citerne. Cross the D112E and continue along the Route de Mantes.

Ruisseau des Ponts-Quentin
Junction on the left with the GR22, heading north-west for 14 kilometres to the Gare d'Orgerus-Behoust.

7Km
1:45

local road down through the pines. Before reaching the valley floor, cross the Chemin Rural du Mesle with the Ducambarderie property on your right. Carry straight on, crossing the D936 and continuing for a further 300 metres.

Go diagonally right on the first track and then turn right onto another track leading to a dolmen, the Pierre Ardoue. Turn left onto the Chemin Rural des Buttes-Rouges and go straight ahead till you reach the corner of the Château de Pincourt.

At the first crossroads, turn right and head towards the Carrefour Bailly. From here, go diagonally left on the Route de Monnerau. At the Carrefour des Ponts-Quentin, cross the Route du Petit et Haut Choisel. Now, descend into the valley carved by the Ruisseau des Ponts-Quentin.

The GR1 bears right and follows the Route aux Vaches to the Etang Rompu. Go round the pool to the left. Now turn left onto the path towards the D138 for 100 metres before turning right onto the Route de l'Etang-Rompu. At the Carrefour Saint-Ruffin, cut across the Route de Bluche and then the Route des Cuisines-de-Monseigneur.

Turn left onto the Route Belsédène. Cross the Route Goron at the Carrefour Belsédène and the Route Tourette at the Carrefour des Maurus. You now come to the Etang de Porte-Baudet which you pass on the left. Go up the forest road which crosses the Route du Haut-Cornu at the Carrefour des Brûlins. Continue straight ahead till you come to the Etang de la Plaine.

Branch left and follow the pool. Leave the Fort de Rambouillet and turn right onto the Rue de Sanc which brings you directly to Montfort-l'Amaury. At the crossroads, turn left up a steep slope and then right into the Rue Maurice Ravel (museum on your left). This brings you to the Rue Saint-Laurent.

Montfort-l'Amaury

This ancient town is built on the slopes of a hill on the northern edge of the Forêt de Rambouillet. The name derives from the feudal house of Montfort, one of whose members, Amaury, gave his name to the place in the 11th century. During the 14th century, the town was attached to the Duchy of Brittany as a result of the marriage of a Montfort to the Breton duke, Arthur. With the marriage of Anne of Brittany to Charles VIII and then to Louis XII, it became part of the kingdom of France. Since 1899, the town has been a place of pilgrimage for the Bretons of Paris, who hold a procession here every year at the beginning of June. Victor Hugo lived here in 1825. The composer Maurice Ravel lived here from 1921 until his death in 1937: his little villa, Le Belvédère, has today been turned into a museum.

The church was built in the 15th century and embellishments continued to the 17th century. The façade and the tower were restored in the last century. See the Renaissance windows and lateral façades. Of the ruined castle, all that remains is part of the 10th-century keep and the Anne of Britanny tower, which dates from the beginning of the Renaissance.

MONTFORT-L'AMAURY

Turn right into the Rue Saint-Laurent and pass under the Porte Bardoul. Now, turn right into the Rue de la Croix-Buisée and right again into the Rue Saint-Nicholas. Turn left onto a steeply climbing gravel track which comes out onto an asphalt road. Turn left and then right. You now reach the D76 (Gare de Montfort 2km left). Cross the road and continue straight ahead. Turn left into the Rue François-Quesnay and then left again into the Rue Léopold-Bellan. This brings you to Méré.

MÉRÉ

Detour *30 mins from the Gare de Montfort-l'Amaury.*

Detour see left. Go straight ahead on the D76 and cross the N12. From here, there are two possibilities:
- towards Rambouillet: continue on the D76. GR1 waymarkings on the right after 2 kilometres. Return to the GR1 on the right.
- towards Neauphle: begin in the same way but turn left off the D76 some 600 metres from the station just before a large warehouse. (The dirt road that you take is not marked on the IGN 1:50,000 map). After 500 metres, turn off to the right onto a minor road which brings you to the church. Turn left into the Rue de Mareil and return to the GR1 on the left.

2.5Km
0:40

Turn right on the GR1 into the Rue Bocquet. Leave the village on a road which heads east, passing under electricity cables. Ignore a track to the right, leading to Mareil-le-Guyon. Cross a minor road linking the N12 to Mareil-le-Guyon.

Junction on the right with the GR11 coming from Coignières.

The GR1 and the GR11 share the same route until they leave Neauphle-le-Vieux.

Continue in the same direction and then cross the N12.

5Km
1:20

Warning Very dangerous crossroads. Go past the Ferme de Saint-Aubin. The GR crosses the railway line and continues straight on into Neauphle-le-Vieux.

NEAUPHLE-LE-VIEUX

At the Place de l'Eglise, turn right onto the Rue de Versailles (D11) and cross the bridge over the Mauldre. Now, turn left into the Rue Charles-de-Gaulle, which brings you to the N191.

1Km
0:20

N191
Detour *10 mins from the Gare Villiers-Neauphle.*

Detour see left. Turn right after a few metres into the Rue de Beynes (N191). Follow the waymarkers, which are white and red with white stripes. After about 200 metres, the N191 intersects with the GR1.

Go straight ahead on the Rue Charles-de-Gaulle to the railway line. Before the level crossing, turn left.

Junction with the GR11 Vallée de la Bièvre.

Follow the railway line for about 200 metres till you come to a short tunnel. The GR11 continues straight ahead towards Orgerus and Mantes.

The GR1 goes through the tunnel on the right and then turns left onto the track to the left. This brings you to the road from Villiers-Saint-Frédéric to Cressay. Turn left here and then right after 50 metres. When you come to a crossroads, go straight over and cross the road linking Neauphle-le-Château to Saint-Germain-de-la-Grange.

6Km
1:45

Turn right onto a track down towards the road.

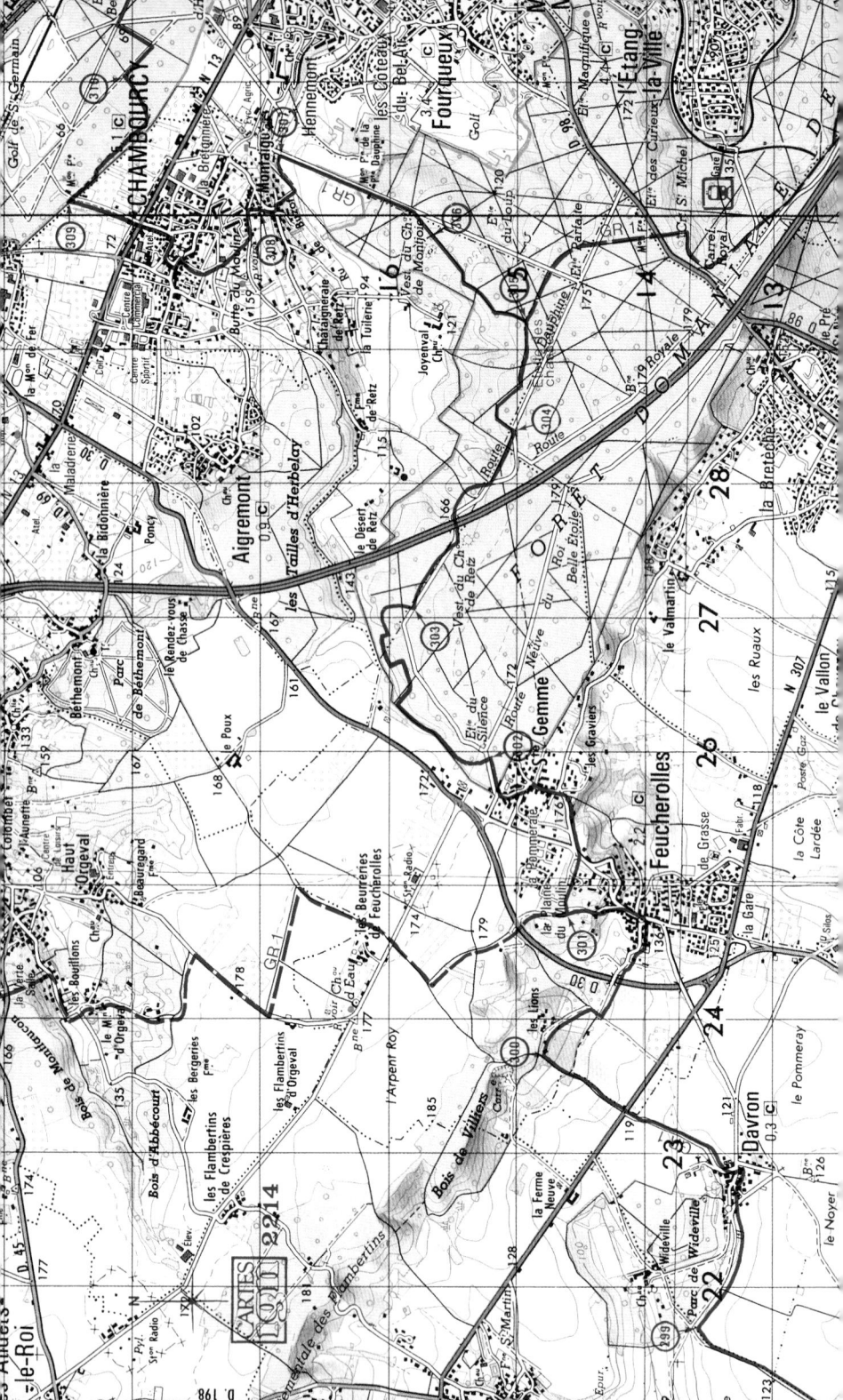

Carry straight on and go over two level crossings. When you come to a junction, do not continue right on the same track and ignore also the left turn. Instead, go almost directly ahead on a farm track, which brings you to the channel of the Ru Mal Droit by a large willow tree.

Note The path is not always easy to see because of ploughing in winter and crops in the summer. Nevertheless, do not hesitate to use it.

After crossing the channel, continue along a track which rises gradually to a crossroads. Turn right and then go down to the left into Thiverval-Grignon.

THIVERVAL-GRIGNON
✕

This commune is the home of the Ecole National d'Agriculture. The school, housed since 1827 in a 17th-century chateau which had in earlier times belonged to the financier Law and to Marshal Bessières, is surrounded by 295 hectares of grounds. Thiverval was also the birthplace of Bartholomé, the creator of the war memorial in the Paris cemetery of Père Lachaise.

3.5Km
1:00

Go through the village and then, beyond the wash-house, turn right onto a track which brings you to the edge of the Parc du Château de Wideville. Turn right to reach Davron.

DAVRON
The Château de Wideville, dating from the 17th century, is a fine building in stone and brick. In the grounds, there is a grotto decorated with shell-work. Visitors may ask the owner's permission to visit at least the grounds.

4Km
1:00

In Davron, turn left onto a road which crosses the N307. Carry straight on along the dirt road towards coppices. At the top of the slope, follow the track which bends to the right. Pass by a place called Les Lions and then descend to a crossroads. Turn left onto the D30 bypass to reach Feucherolles.

FEUCHEROLLES
✕ ⛪

See the 12th-century church with its romanesque tower, gothic statuary and modern

Turn left at the church and come onto the D30 again. Follow the road for 100 metres to the mairie, where you turn left on a road going up towards the woods. At the top of the hill, you come to a crossroads.

0.5Km 0:10	*windows. Ask for the key at the mairie.*

Crossroads

The GR1 continues straight on from here towards Triel, going first north and then northwest.

1.5Km 0:20

To go towards Paris or Achères, turn east onto a track. Cross the D30 and go straight ahead on the road to Sainte-Gemme.

SAINTE-GEMME

In the village, turn left, left again and then right. You come to the south-west tip of the Forêt de Marly at the Maison Forestière de Sainte-Gemme and then continue from there.

At the Etoile du Silence, ignore the Route Forestière de La Mare à La Bonde, which goes right. Instead, turn left onto a track which winds through the valley and climbs up again to the Etoile du Précipice, close to the road. Turn left onto a path through woods thick with bracken (so thick in summer that it can block the way and conceal waymarkers). Beyond a clearing, the track goes down into a valley and up the other side.

5.5Km 1:30

From the Etoile de la Grande-Jument, follow the closely spaced waymarkers through the forest. Pass under the A13 autoroute and turn left onto a gravel track. After 50 metres, turn right onto a forest track. Pass the Etoile Descente and come to the Route Dauphine. Immediately turn off left onto another forest road. Two right turns will now bring you to the Route des Chasseurs, which leads to the Etoile des Chasseurs.

Etoile des Chasseurs
Junction with the eastern branch of the GR1, which continues straight on east towards Marly-le-Roi and the Porte Maillot.

If you are coming from Sainte-Gemme and want to head for Saint-Germain and Achères, turn left (north) and then go diagonally right (north-east) along a wide avenue.

Cross a road leading to the ruins of Montjoie.

Detour
Château de Montjoie.
The château derives its name from the location, formerly known as Mons Jovis.

Detour see left. Take the track on the left for 150 metres before turning off right into the bushes.

Go down to the Route des Princesses, passing

4.5Km
1:10

Nothing now remains but some embanked ground covered with vegetation. The original fortress, built by Clovis, later became one of the largest castles in France. It belonged to the Abbaye de Saint-Denis and this explains the famous battle-cry, 'Saint-Denis et Montjoie'. The castle played an important role in the Hundred Years' War but was devastated after the Battle of Azincourt. In 1690, it was finally demolished by Louis XIV to remove an obstruction to the hunt.

CHAMBOURCY

Picturesque village on a hillside. 12th-century church. Cemetery with graves of the famous dandy, the Chevalier d'Orsay, and of the painter, André Derain.

Forêt Domaniale de Saint-Germain

The 4,000 hectare forest is planted with hornbeam, oak, beech and chestnut. The GR follows winding bridle paths.

7Km
1:45

the Maison Forestière de la Porte Dauphine. Make a 90 degree turn left onto a grassy track. Follow a stream and a wire fence. Go through a large gap in the tumble down wall (Le Ru de Buzot). Turn right and go up towards Montaigu. In the hamlet, turn left and then go right at the first crossroads.

At the first bend, turn left on the track leading up to the plateau. Turn left and then right. Go through a property and then down towards the cemetery. Carry straight on with walls on either side. The road now brings you to Chambourcy.

In the Place de l'Eglise, turn left into the Grande-Rue and then continue on the Rue Chaude. Take a right turn and then a left. Cross the N13 and carry straight on. Pass through orchards to the Porte de Chambourcy, the entrance to the state forest of Saint-Germain.

Once through the Porte de Chambourcy, turn right and follow the forest wall. Continue along a footpath. Cross one track and, when you come to the next, turn left. At the Etoile de la Reine, go diagonally right and then left to reach the Etoile de Beaumont. Go across and turn right onto a paved avenue, following the path on the left-hand side. Cross an avenue.

Turn left and head towards a level crossing. Go over and immediately turn left onto a footpath, which brings you to a large crossroads. Cross the N184 and then the N190. Follow the fence on your right. Opposite the Camp de Loges, turn right off the road and take the track between the municipal stadium of Saint-Germain and a reafforestation area. Turn left onto a path through coppices for 1 kilometre. Cross the N284 and carry on for another 600 metres.

Turn left and then go right at the Etoile du

Petit-Parc. Follow the Route du Petit-Parc across two roads until you come to the gate of the wall which once enclosed the Terrasse de Saint-Germain.

Terrasse de Saint-Germain
Detour *25 mins*
from the
GARE RER DE SAINT-GERMAIN-EN-LAYE

Detour see left. Take the exit marked Place du Château-Rue de la Paroisse. When you come out from the steps, cross the road and go through the gate at the corner of the château. Go diagonally left along the first avenue towards the terrace. Follow the terrace north to go through a door in the wall separating the terrace from the forest. You will now find the GR waymarkings: straight ahead to Chambourcy; right for Achères-Ville.

The GR follows a track parallel to the terrace wall. With your back to the Royal Gate, turn right onto a path leading down to the D157. Cross the road and take the steps up to the Château du Val. Turn left and cross the esplanade to the Grande Clairière. Turn right onto a path leading to the Etoile d'Actéon. Turn left off the path onto a track for riders and head towards the Mare aux Canes.

6.5Km
1:40

The GR1 follows the water for a few metres. After the first path to the right, it joins a straight avenue leading to the N184. Now turn right and come to the Etoile de Bon-Secours. Head north-east on another footpath through a newly planted area. Cross the La Muette training track and turn left on a path which is also

Terrasse de Saint-Germain

The Terrasse de Saint-Germain was designed by Le Nôtre and completed in 1673. It took 4 years of immense works to construct the terrace, which is 30m wide and 2,400m long. The lime trees were planted in 1745. From here, there is a remarkable view over the valley of the Seine and all the western suburbs of Paris.

Saint-Germain was founded in the reign of Dagobert. It was often the home of the kings of France and it was here that Louis XIV was born. In more modern times, it was the terminus of the first railway line. The château, rebuilt under Francis I, houses the national collection of antiquities for the prehistoric, Celtic and Gallo-Roman periods. Visit the Eglise Saint-Louis, the Musée du Prieuré and the municipal museum. which has Hieronymus Bosch's painting 'L'Escamoteur'.

used by riders. Turn right and then, when you come to the Etoile de Vaux, turn left to the Etoile du Chêne-Corbeau. Head diagonally right towards the Etoile des Amazones on the N308. Cross over and take the forest road opposite for 200 metres to the Route Monsieur.

Route Monsieur
Detour *30 mins*
GARE DE MAISONS-LAFITTE
🏠 ✕ 🚉 🚌 🚂
Visit the château and the grounds of Maisons-Lafitte.

Detour see left. Turn right on a combined footpath-bridlepath towards Maisons-Lafitte. After 200 metres, turn left onto the Route du Mesnil. About half-way, intersect for the first time with the Circuit PR11 de Maisons-Lafitte (orange waymarkers). Now turn right onto the Route du Lude. Leave the forest through the Porte Blanche. Carry on before turning left outside a block of flats. Turn right into the Rue Saint-Nicholas and continue straight ahead until you come to the station car park.

2.5Km
0:45

At the junction with the Route de Monsieur, take a footpath bearing off to the left.

For 200 metres, just before the Avenue de la Muette, the GR1 and the Circuit PR11 de Maisons-Lafitte share the same route.

Cross the La Muette training track again. Turn right into a forest avenue. Pass by, on your right the second 30 minute detour to Maisons-Lafitte. After the beech grove, turn off diagonally right onto an avenue leading to the Etoile du Chêne-Capitaine.

Etoile du Chêne-Capitaine
Detour *25 mins*
from the Gares d'Achères-Grand-Cormier.
This elegant hunting lodge was built by Gabriel in the reign of Louis XV, replacing an earlier one dating from the times of Francis I.

Turn left and cross the road between the forest pavilions. Go into the forest on a path at a 45° angle to the two roads. When you reach the Croix-Saint-Simon, turn left onto the track along the Achères training field, which brings you to the Etoile du Chêne-Capitaine. Cross a bridge and carry on along an avenue of chestnut trees.

Cross the forest road, which leads left to Achres or right to Maisons-Lafitte. Continue straight on towards the Pavillon de la Muette.

Junction with the PR11 de Maisons-Lafitte (orange waymarkers). The GR1 and

Go round the pavilion on the left and then follow the fencing of a newly planted enclosure. After two right angle turns to the

■
3Km
0:45

PR11 share the same route for 3 kilometres

left, turn your back to the enclosure and head directly west. Turn left onto a broader avenue between the Maison Forestière de l'Etoile du Loup and the Etoile de la Sablonnière to the right. After 300 metres, the GR moves onto a narrow winding path for about 250 metres. This leads out onto a wide avenue, beneath which runs the pipeline bringing gas from Holland to the underground reservoir of Beynes. Turn left onto the avenue for 500 metres. Go past the Maison Forestière de l'Etoile du Loup and cross a disused road.

Disused road
Starting point of 2nd detour from the Gare d'Achères-Grand-Cormier.
Detour *15 mins*
from the Gare d'Achères-Grand-Cormier

1.5Km
0:20

The PR11, with its orange waymarkers, shares the same route as the GR1.

Outside the station, cross the concrete bridge and go down the steps. Go through the wood diagonally opposite, crossing the forest road between Achères to the left and Maisons-Lafitte to the right. Continue straight ahead for 50 metres and then enter the wood on the left. Go along the edge of a pond and cross an avenue. This will bring you to the road that can be seen on the right. Here, you meet the GR: opposite is the section coming from Saint-Germain; to the left is the section going to the Gare Nouvelle d'Achères-Ville.

Go past the avenue with the gas pipeline on the left and continue straight ahead, crossing the N184. When you come to a fairly wide track, turn right. 200 metres beyond the Etoile du Maine, take the path which follows the edge of the forest to the left. Go diagonally left to reach a cemetery and the Gare d'Achères-Ville.

Gare d'Achères-Ville

Beyond this point, there are no waymarkers. However, walkers who wish to continue on the GR1 without going through Paris can go to Cergy-Pontoise on Line A of the RER and then on to Pontoise by bus. From there, continue on foot towards Auvers-sur-Oise and L'Isle-Adam.

WALK 2

VIARMES
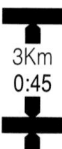

3Km
0:45

The GR1A starts out from Asnières-sur-Oise but it is better to begin 3 kilometres earlier, from Viarmes.

ASNIÈRES-SUR-OISE

Church, dating from the 11th and 13th centuries, with an octagonal tower.

The starting point of the GR1A is situated next to the last property in the village. Coming from Viarmes, the GR1 turns left and climbs slightly as it heads towards Noisy-sur-Oise. The GR1A turns right and comes into the village down the Rue de l'Orme. After a crossroads, go straight along the Rue de Gouvieux to the D922, where you turn left and continue for 50 metres. Now turn right and come to the Carrefour Balettre.

4.5Km
1:10

Instead of crossing the D922 deviation, follow it left for 500 metres, going through a tunnel. Turn left onto a dirt road leading to another crossroads near the D922.

Turn right onto a dirt road which later veers right towards the Oise. It comes out near a pumping station onto a minor road.

Minor road
The minor road links the bypass connection to a dam on the Oise.
Detour *30 mins along the PR path*
Abbaye de Royaumont

Detour see left. Follow the minor road to the right for 250 metres to the PR, which continues left for 1.8 kilometres on a track across country to the famous Abbaye de Royaumont.

3Km
0:45

This Cistercian monastery, founded by Saint Louis in 1228, prospered greatly until the Revolution. In 1971, the church was largely destroyed and the buildings were converted into a cotton mill. After various other vicissitudes, the place became a centre for cultural exchanges. It is well worth visiting to see the remarkable 13th-century cloister and refectory.

The GR1A now turns left. Approaching the dam, it bears right and crosses the bridge over the Thève. You now follow the Oise and go over another bridge. The dirt road continues between fields on the left and woods, pasture and fallow land on the right. Immediately after a pumping station, turn left onto a track towards the Plage de Boran, where the bar and swimming pool are open every day from May to September. Turn left and cross the Oise by the bridge of Boran-sur-Oise.

BORAN-SUR-OISE
🏛 ✕ 🚂 🚌

The church, dating from the 13th and 16th centuries, has an unusual spire with crockets.

2.5Km
0:45

Ferme de Morancy

4Km
1:00

Junction of five roads
Detour *10 mins*
Précy-sur-Oise
✕ 🚂 🚌

Church, dating from the 13th and 14th centuries, with splendid rose-window and carved stone altar-piece.

4Km
1:00

Blaincourt
16th-century church.

The GR does not enter the town, instead turning right after the bridge and continuing along the towpath to the vicinity of the new concrete works.

Turn left and go over the level crossing. Take a track running parallel to a private road, which you go under through a little tunnel. Carry straight on parallel to the railway track for 600 metres. Now turn left and go up towards a little wood. Cross the D603 and continue ahead on a road leading to the Ferme de Morancy.

The GR now goes right on a dirt road up to the plateau. You soon come to the shaft of an old stone cross where a track comes in from the left. Carry straight on to an electricity pylon.

Warning No waymarkers.

300 metres beyond the pylon, turn off to the right on a dirt road. After 200 metres, turn left and then, 250 metres further on, go right again. Cross a gravel road. Now continue towards a workman's hut and out onto the plateau. Cross the D92 and carry straight on to the junction of five roads.

Descend along a sunken lane. Turn left into the Rue du Docteur Charles-Andrieux and then right into the Allée Henri-Youf, which brings you to the Place de l'Eglise. Take the second road on the left to reach the station. Now turn left. After 1 kilometre, you come onto another dirt road. Follow this for 250 metres to a minor road, on which you go straight ahead.

After a little wood, turn right onto a dirt road down to Blaincourt. Go right here for 50 metres on the D44. Turn left onto the Chemin du Sonage and then left again onto the Chemin des Erolles. This brings you onto the Rue Madeleine-Hobigand, which leads to the the church of Blaincourt.

The GR now turns right and follows the Rue des Sablons up towards the Bois de la Brosse.

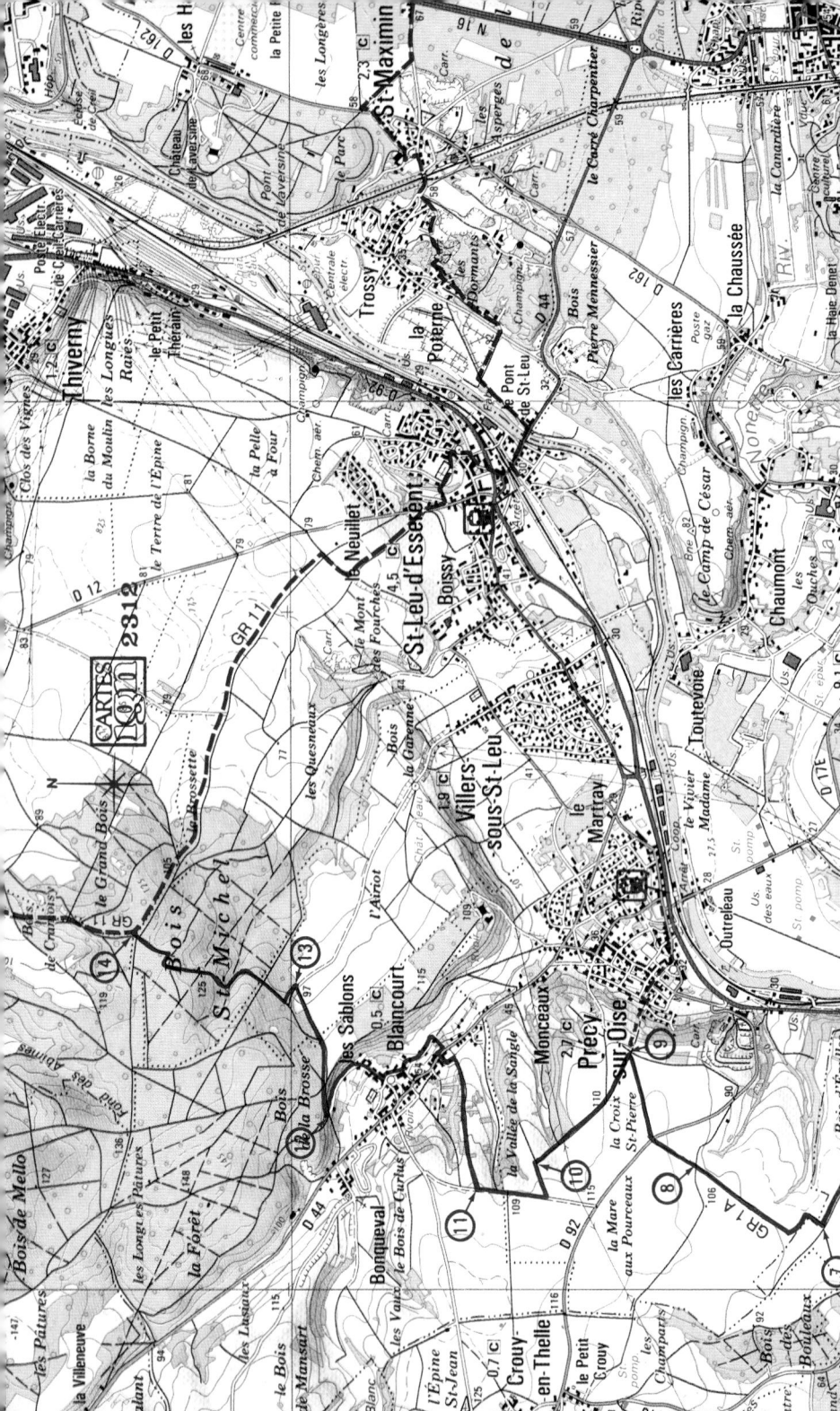

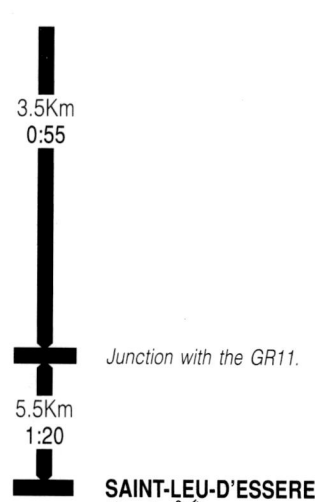

3.5Km
0:55

At a junction near a property, turn right onto a track leading into the woods. On the other side, the GR skirts the wood until it reaches a minor road coming from Villers-sous-Saint-Leu.

Turn left and go into the Bois Saint-Michel.

Warning As the route now changes direction and altitude markedly, do not leave the waymarked path. The GR goes past a huntsman's cabin and reaches the GR11.

Junction with the GR11.

5.5Km
1:20

A left turn here will take you towards Maysel and Cires-lès-Mello. If you turn right, the GR will bring you to the Gare de Saint-Leu-d'Esserent.

SAINT-LEU-D'ESSERENT

WALK 3

The GR1B, which links the GR1 and GR11, allows the rambler a one-day walk from the stations of Lizy-sur-Ourcq or Isles-Armentières to the station at Meaux. The reason for doing the walk in this direction is the small number of trains on the La Ferté-Milon line. The route to the GR1B is described below.

The first section of the route, from Villers-lès-Rigault to Varreddes, can be walked at any time of year as it follows gravel tracks and then the towpath along the Ourcq. The latter part, from Varreddes to Crégy-lès-Meaux, should only be attempted in clear, dry weather – the tracks are very muddy – while the main interest lies in the views over the Marne as it meanders round a succession of villages.

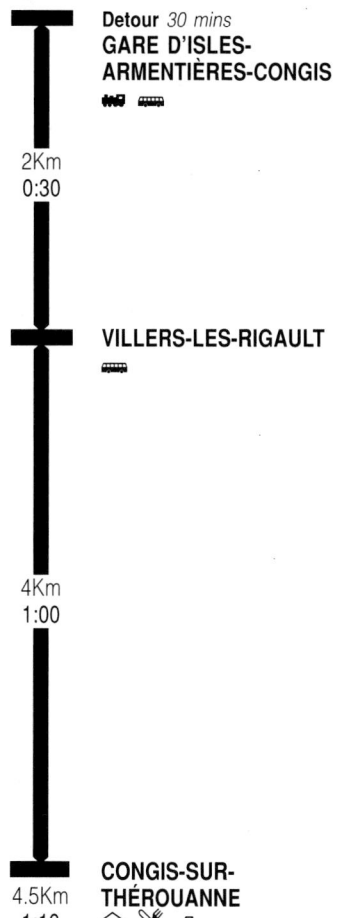

Detour *30 mins*
GARE D'ISLES-ARMENTIÈRES-CONGIS

2Km
0:30

Outside the station, follow the waymarkers of the GR11 to the right on the D17E. Then turn left into the Rue de Trilport (D17). After the war memorial, turn right into a road leading to the old church square. Walk down a grassy track to the road and cross the Marne. Now turn right into the Rue du Grand-Voyeux. After 100 metres, turn left into an avenue lined with poplars. Turn right onto the canal bank and continue till you come to a bridge marking the starting point of the GR1B.

VILLERS-LES-RIGAULT

The GR11 turns right onto the towpath. The GR1B crosses the Canal de l'Ourcq. 150 metres after the canal bridge, it turns left onto a gravel track and continues into an acacia wood. Carry on for 1 kilometre along the main track. As you leave the wood, turn left onto a dirt road and cross the canal.

4Km
1:00

Turn right onto the towpath, leading to the D121 at the entry to the village of Congis. Turn right onto this road to cross the canal. Now turn left onto a track parallel to the canal, curving round into the Vallon de la Thérouanne.

At a T-junction, turn left. Cross the River Thérouanne and its headrace before going up onto the plateau. Near a cemetery, pick up a road which crosses the Canal de l'Ourcq at the entry to Congis-sur-Thérouanne.

4.5Km
1:10
CONGIS-SUR-THÉROUANNE

Turn right onto the towpath. After 3 kilometres, you come to the D405 on the way into Varreddes.

12th-century church.

VARREDDES

ⓗ ✕ ⛲ 🚌

The 13th-century church was restored in the 16th century. Inside, there are several tombstones, including that of the poet Nicholas Yveteaux, tutor to the children of Henri IV and Gabrielle d'Estrées and then to Louis XIII.

Junction on the left with the PR4 d'Isles-les-Meldeuses.

10Km
2:30

Go right on the D405. Cross a canal and turn left onto a track parallel to the bank. After 50 metres, turn left onto another track. Shortly afterwards, turn right onto a track leading into a wood. When you come out, continue along the edge, rounding the tip of the wood on a footpath which takes you to a dirt road. Turn left here. On the plateau, go past a track leading off to the right.

At a junction without waymarkers, turn left on a grassy track leading towards a wood. Come out on a bend in the D97. Turn right along this road for 100 metres and then take a dirt road on the left, which follows the edge of a wood. A little further on, you come first to a German and then to a French cemetery of the 1914-1918 war. On the right, there is a viewpoint looking out towards the Buttes de Penchard and the Buttes de Bois d'Automne. In the distance, you can see the Butte de Monthyon with the Roissy radar station. Opposite, there is the massive tower of the Cathédrale de Meaux.

Follow the walking instructions carefully as there are no waymarkers at intersections.

Continue south on the track for 1.2 kilometres, enjoying views over various villages in the bends of the Marne. The GR bends right. At the next intersection, continue straight ahead between fields and orchards. Cross the Route de Chambry and carry on ahead for 1.2 kilometres. Follow a path through a copse along a fence (the track here is regularly ploughed up and sown by the owner of the adjoining field). The track now descends towards the plain of Meaux. The cathedral can be seen beyond the Bois Saint-Faron. To the left are the new developments of Beauval and La Pierre-Collinet. To the right is Le Vieux Crégy.

Turn sharp right to go back up to the plateau. Follow the edge of the wood. After 800 metres, bear diagonally left. At a junction without waymarkers, turn left towards the edge of the plateau and then right towards a little wood.

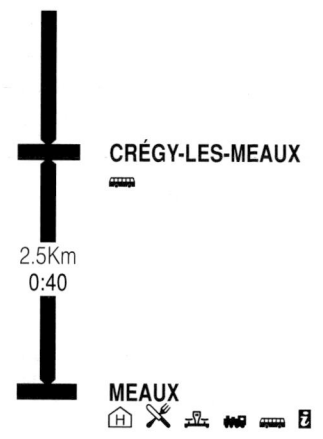

CRÉGY-LES-MEAUX

2.5Km
0:40

MEAUX

Continue straight ahead along the edge of the plateau and vegetable gardens before coming onto the Chemin des Buttes at the entry to Crégy-lès-Meaux.

Follow this road into the village and past the church. Turn right and come into the Rue Roger-Salengro.

Junction with the GR1 where the road forks. Bear left on the Rue de la Roche and the GR1 will bring you to the station in the centre of Meaux.

WALK 4

The GR1C links Poigny-la-Forêt on the GR1 with the GR11. Coming from Montfort-l'Amaury, follow the edge of the Etang du Roi on your left. At the end, carry straight on along a minor road, leading to Poigny-la-Forêt.

If you are coming from Rambouillet, turn right off the Route de la Mouche when you reach the Etang du Roi and take a minor road towards Poigny-la Forêt.

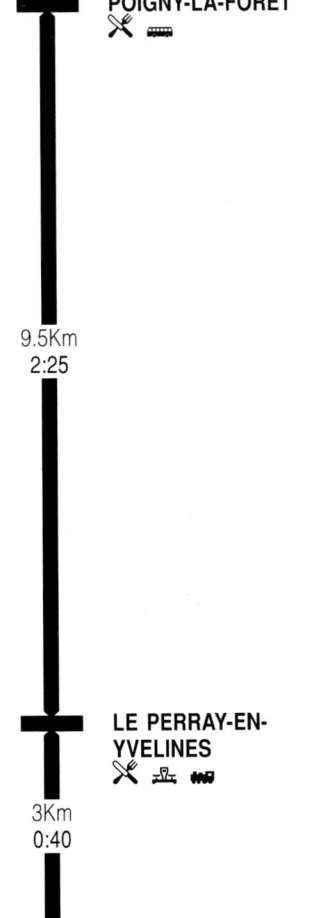

POIGNY-LA-FORÊT

The road follows the River Guesle. Turn left onto the D107 and continue for about 1 kilometre. Turn right and cross the D936. Carry on uphill as far as the Propriété des Fainiers. Turn right onto a narrow path, which leads you to a forest road. Go right here and then turn off left onto a track leading to the Carrefour du Hallier. Turn left here onto another track, which crosses the Route Ducambard about 300 metres further on.

Go right on the Route de Rambouillet for a few metres and then turn off onto a path almost opposite. Follow the edge of the Etang du Coupe-Gorge and then turn left onto a road which goes round it. Where the road bears left, turn your back to the pool and go down to the right on a path which joins the Chemin de la Grande-Brèche. Follow this road for a good kilometre. You now emerge from the forest on the outskirts of Perray-en-Yvelines. Follow the Grande Rue-Verte, the Croix-Barbé and the Petite Rue-Verte to a crossroads. Turn right and come to the D910. Go straight across into a street leading to the Gare du Perray-en-Yvelines.

9.5Km
2:25

LE PERRAY-EN-YVELINES

Take the subway and then turn left onto a road following the railway track. Turn right onto a path following the left bank of the Etang du Perray. Carry straight on and then turn off on a road to the right. Paying close attention to the waymarkers, turn left onto a sunken lane, which brings you to the edge of a meadow. Turn right onto a road leading to Auffargis.

3Km
0:40

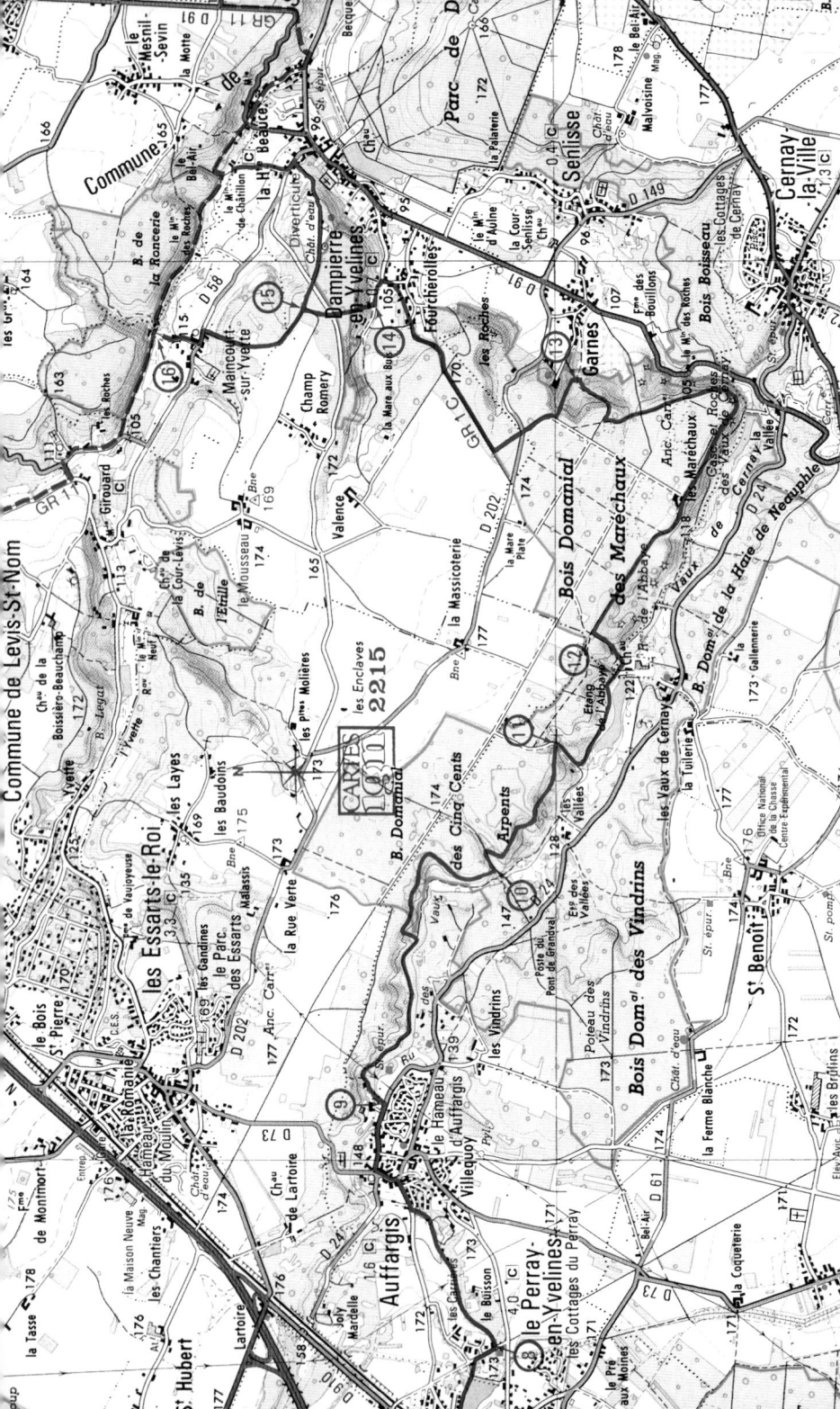

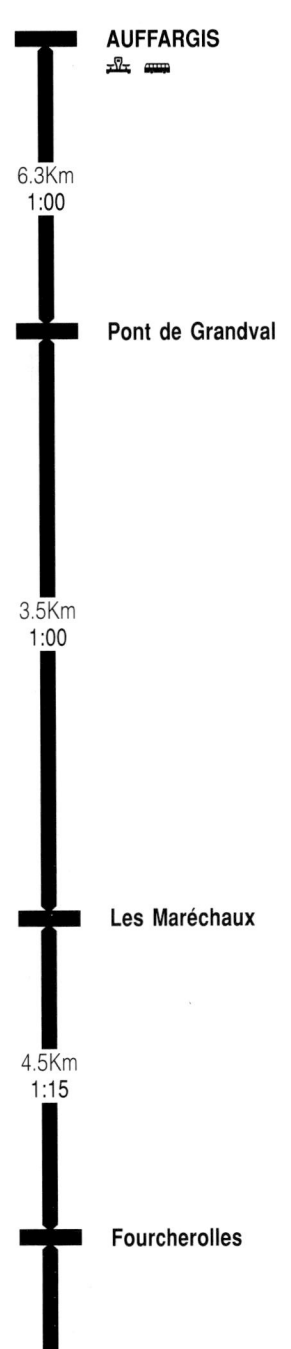

AUFFARGIS

6.3Km
1:00

Pont de Grandval

3.5Km
1:00

Les Maréchaux

4.5Km
1:15

Fourcherolles

Take the main road through the village. Turn right at the church and follow the D24 for 300 metres.

At the entry to a one-way street, turn into a lane leading between pavilions and fenced off properties. Further on, turn off to the left on a path at right angles leading to the summit of the Buttes d'Auffargis. Zig-zag down a path to the Pont de Grandval.

Before the bridge, turn left and take a steep path up to the top of the hill. Continue almost straight ahead on a winding road. Go down to the right on the Côte des Jumelles. At the bottom, turn left onto a track which brings you to the Abbaye de Cernay.

Founded in 1118 by the Benedictines but was later taken over by the Cistercian order. The ruins, dating from the latter half of the 12th century, rise up starkly from the green of the valley floor. In the background stands a façade (1190) of the former abbey church. This scene of wild beauty is one of the major attractions of the walk.

Turn off diagonally left to the Bois de Vieille-Bonde. At the end of the track, by a large beech, branch right on a path, which leads to a jumble of rocks. An avenue now brings you to the houses of Les Maréchaux.

This is the starting point for a path along the edge of the Vaux de Cernay. Turn left and reach the promontory of Mont Pelouse. Pay close attention to the waymarkers on the way down to a small clearing with outcropping sandstone. The path now comes to a hill planted with pines. Go down the other side to a clearing marked out by the buildings of a *colonie de vacances*. Go up the path and across the D202. Further on, bear right on an avenue leading to Fourcherolles.

After crossing a small river, turn left. Head right till you come to a sunken lane. This goes up through a very gullied stretch and continues on an avenue which takes you to the road between Dampierre and Essarts. Cross the

Chateau de Dampierre

2Km
0:30

road and continue ahead on a narrow track between wire fences. This brings you to a junction and the detour on the right to La Maison de Fer.

LA MAISON DE FER

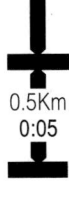

Detour *10 mins*
Turn right onto a path leading to the water tower. A path on the right leads down to Dampierre.

Detour *15 mins*
Moulin de Châtillon

Beyond La Maison de Fer, a second detour leads down to the D58. It turns first left and then right towards the Moulin de Châtillon. Close by the latter, it joins the GR11: turn right for Chevreuse, left for Coignières.

1Km
0:15

Maincourt-sur-Yvette

0.5Km
0:05

Junction with the GR11.

After a minor road, the GR1C turns left on a track leading to Maincourt-sur-Yvette.

At the D58, turn left and then, shortly afterwards, right. Go down towards the Marais de l'Yvette as far as the lodge.

Go left to Coignières (5 kilometres), right to Saint-Rémy-lès-Chevreuse (8 kilometres).

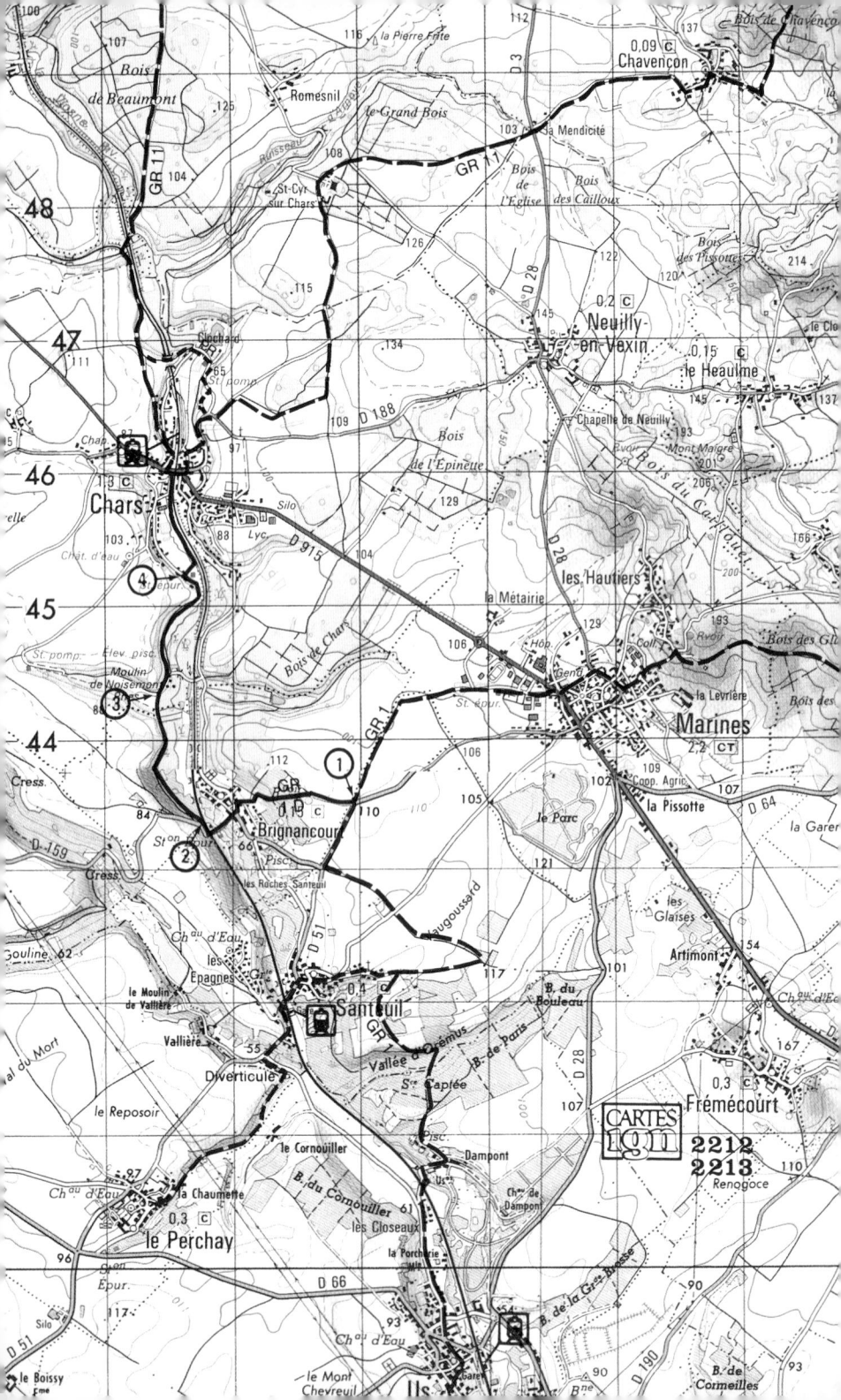

WALK 5

This pleasant link between Brignancourt (GR1) and Chars (GR11), provides an extension to the Meulan-Santeuil section (21km).

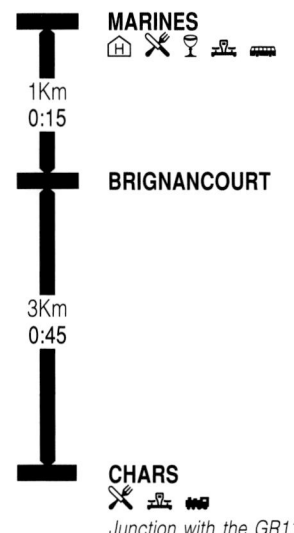

MARINES

1Km
0:15

The starting point of the GR is on the D159, 2 kilometres to the west of Marines. The GR heads west towards the entry to a wood. A winding gravel track takes you down from here to Brignancourt.

BRIGNANCOURT

3Km
0:45

Follow the Rue de la Mairie to the Place des Tilleuls. Turn left and then right. The GR crosses first the River Viosne and then the railway. Where the road bends left, continue straight ahead on a very muddy track under trees. After a meadow, take the track to the right. Before a sewage treatment plant, turn right towards the railway. Continue on a track parallel to the railway line until you come to a level crossing at Chars.

CHARS

Junction with the GR11.

ACCOMMODATION GUIDE

The many different kinds of accommodation in France are explained in the introduction. Here we include a selection of hotels and other addresses, which is by no means exhaustive – the hotels listed are usually in the one-star or two-star categories. We have given full postal addresses where available so bookings can be made.

There has been an explosive growth in bed and breakfast facilities (chambres d'hôte) in the past few years, and staying in these private homes can be especially interesting and rewarding. Local shops and the town hall (mairie) can usually direct you to one.

Bonnelles
78830
⌂ *Louveterie du Château*
Mr Mariton
☎ *(1) 30.41.47.18*

Chaumes-en-Brie
77390 Seine-et-Marne
⌂ *La Chaum'yerres*
Mr and Mme Berton
☎ *(1) 64.06.03.42*

Crécy-la-Chapelle
77580 Seine-et-Marne
⌂ *Auberge du Pont de Villiers*
Mr Laporte
☎ *(1) 64.36.92.15*
☎ *(1) 64.35.83.97*

Ermenonville
60950 Oise
⌂ *De la Croix d'Or*
Mr Vezier
☎ *44.54.00.04*

Fontainebleau
77300 Seine-et-Marne
⌂ *A la Carpe d'Or*
Mr Badee
☎ *(1) 64.22.28.64*
⌂ *De l'Ile de France*
Mr Glise
☎ *64.22.21.17*
⌂ *Le Richelieu*
Mr Marin
☎ *(1) 64.22.26.46*

Gazeran
78120 Rambouillet
⌂ *Auberge Villa Marinette*
Mr Kieger
☎ *(1) 34.83.19.01*
Le Perchay
⌂ *Ferme de la Tanière*
Mr Millecamps
☎ *(1) 34.66.04.25*

Les Hauts-Besnières
78720 La Celle-les-Bordes
⌂ *Maison du Parc Naturel*
☎ *(1) 30.52.09.09*

L'Isle-Adam
95290
⌂ *Centre Nature de l'Isle-de-Champagne*
☎ *(1) 34.69.03.55*

Maisons-Lafitte
78600 Yvelines
⌂ *Auberge d'Alencon*
Mr Topart
☎ *39.12.19.99*

Malesherbes
45330 Loiret
⌂ *Ecu de France*
Mr Grosmangin
☎ *38.34.87.25*

Montfort-l'Amaury
78490 Yvelines
⌂ *Des Voyageurs*

Mme Renard
☎ *(1) 34.86.00.14*

Vernouillet
28500 Eure-et-Loir
⌂ *Auberge de la Vallée Verte*
Mr Paille
☎ *37.46.04.04*
☎ *37.42.54.71*

Viarmes
95270
⌂ *Des Amis de la Nature*
☎ *(1) 30.35.81.82*
☎ *(1) 30.35.87.22*

INDEX

Details of train connections from Paris have been provided wherever it was possible. We suggest you refer also to the map inside the front cover.

INDEX

YOUR KEY TO EXPLORING
FRANCE
ign MAPS

GREEN SERIES 1:100,000
FRANCE IN 74 MAPS

- large scale — 1¼=1 mile
- contours
- all roads graded and numbered
- tracks and GR paths
- key in English

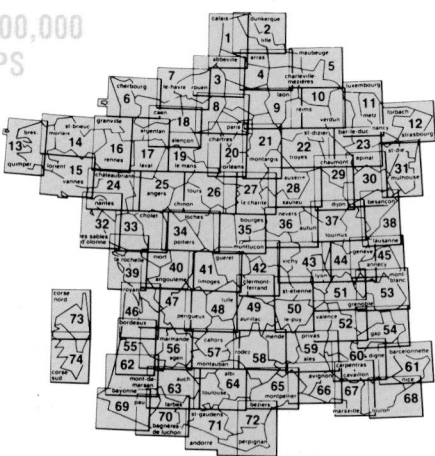

RED SERIES 1:250,000
FRANCE IN 16 MAPS

- The definitive French road maps
- all roads graded and numbered
- distances between towns
- tourist information
- index of places of interest

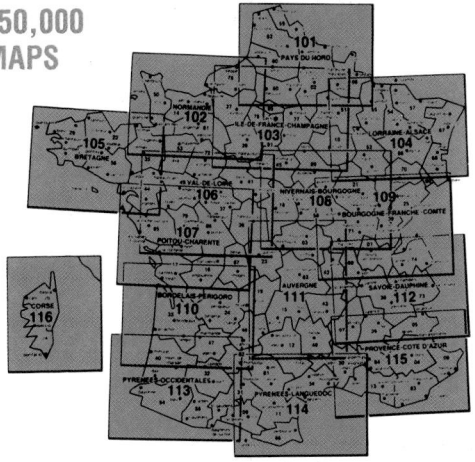

Available from good bookshops everywhere